Praise for
TRANSFORMATIONAL DREAMING

"I loved Jill Morris's TRANSFORMATIONAL DREAMING. It reads like a novel and will become inspiring reading not only for professionals but also for everybody puzzled by the mystery of dreams and their messages in human life. This creatively written book fully confirms my own experience: Working with dreams and emotions can provide decisive and safe access to buried memories. Highly recommended."

—ALICE MILLER
Author of *The Dream of the Gifted Child*

"Jill Morris's TRANSFORMATIONAL DREAMING covers it all, from dreams about AIDS to creative dreams, from nightmares to portents of the future. Dr. Morris's explanations are articulate, her information is authoritative, her exercises are enjoyable, and her examples of breakthrough dreams are unforgettable. The book is so user-friendly that its readers will look forward to putting its insights to use whenever they emerge from dreamtime."

—STANLEY KRIPPNER, Ph.D.
Professor of Psychology
Saybrook Institute

By Jill Morris:

CREATIVE BREAKTHROUGHS
THE DREAM WORKBOOK*
TRANSFORMATIONAL DREAMING*

*Published by Fawcett Books

TRANSFORMATIONAL DREAMING

Jill Morris, Ph.D.

FAWCETT CREST • NEW YORK

6759708

A Fawcett Crest Book
Published by Ballantine Books
Copyright © 1996 by Jill Morris, Ph.D.

Spring Publications, Inc.: Excerpt by C. G. Jung from *Spring*, edited by James Hillman, New York, The Analytical Psychology Club of N.Y., Inc., 1960.

Cover illustration by Jill Morris

http://www.randomhouse.com

Library of Congress Catalog Card Number: 95-96155

ISBN: 0-449-22362-0

Manufactured in the United States of America

First Edition: June 1996

10 9 8 7 6 5 4 3 2 1

"Let's celebrate that we recognize the power of the dream to indicate the turns in the labyrinth."
—Anaïs Nin
from *Credo, A Celebration of Life*

(put together by Renata Brooks for WBAI)

Acknowledgments

My thanks to three wonderful friends who read over my first draft and then offered their invaluable input: Regina Rheinstein, musician and teacher; Julia Scully, writer and editor; and Dr. Selma Skolnick, educator.

To all the dreamers who generously contributed their material to my book: Caren Bayer, Patrick Daniels, Margaret Evangeline, Joan Witkowski, and the others whose identities I have not revealed. And to Bill.

I thank my agent Nancy Love, who helped me shape my proposal into acceptable form and then jokingly offered to take out a contract on anyone who refused to give me one; my dear friend, screenwriter and producer Gina Rubinstein, for her thoughtful editing of my last draft; and my editor, Susan Randol, for her vision and direction.

My thanks also to Linda Trichter-Metcalf, whose workshops opened up new directions in my writing, and to Jeff Cohen.

Chapter Outline

Introduction

Since the beginning of time, people have taken their dreams to heart. Everyone from prophets to kings relied on them as messages from God (or gods), worthy of the utmost respect and awe. Monarchs consulted them for advice on important matters of state, and their revelations often dictated the course of action that was taken. It was commonly believed, and often proven, that disaster awaited those people foolish enough to ignore their dreams' messages. Today, many people regard dreams as parables for their lives and barometers of their feelings. Others perceive them as expressing their deepest buried wishes. Still others see dreams as potent and infinite sources of creativity, or count on them to clarify conflicts and provide solutions to problems. Many people believe dreams emanate from the deep wisdom of the collective unconscious, which is inherited and derived from the collective experience of the species. Dreams are all these things, and much more. It's no mystery that they have the power to transform our lives, *if* we listen to them.

I view dreams as invaluable gifts from the unconscious. No matter how prosaic or terrifying a dream may appear to be, it can always tell us a truth about ourselves or our lives. Big dreams are those that enlighten us. They often address the deep, unresolved

1

traumas that give birth to our lifelong conflicts, and thus prevent us from following what C. G. Jung refers to as the "inner blueprint" of our lives. I call these big dreams "transformative dreams." The truth they tell is so profound that it can steer those of us who have veered off course back on to the right track.

Transformative dreams appear when we are finally ready to see past the lies and distortions we've constructed to avoid pain. We are then able to go beyond the adaptive defenses that prevent us from achieving our full potential. They come at that moment in our lives when we are prepared to hear their message. It might be when we are at an important stage of transition; or it could be that our defenses have been sufficiently eroded by either physical or mental suffering. When we are vulnerable, we are more open to receiving the truth about ourselves and our situations. This help that comes from inside us could very well be the wisest, most productive help we will ever receive.

When people arrive at an impasse in their lives, that point when every idea has been exhausted and every solution has failed, the transformative dream can seem like a miraculous answer from God. "When the need is greatest, then the answer comes sooneth," runs a line from a song in Kurt Weill's *Beggar's Opera*. But there are few hard-and-fast rules in the world of dreams. Some people dream most vividly when life is going smoothly and they are neither particularly elated nor depressed. One thing is certain: if we ignore our dreams we rob ourselves of their invaluable insights and answers.

Sometimes discovering the meaning of just *one* symbol in a dream is all that is needed to transform a person's life. Many people wonder why dreams don't speak directly. They don't understand the reason why dreams disguise their meanings with symbolic language. Freud addressed these issues almost a hundred years ago. The dream, he said, speaks the language of the unconscious. Its purpose is to preserve sleep by obscuring the dream's true meaning, so that the dreamer does not awaken in horror. The dream disguises the blatant wishes, embarrassment, guilt, etc., of the dream's real meaning by depicting a story that seems wholly unrelated to the dream's message. Thus, everything in the dream is really a symbol for something else. Through his theory, Freud provided the foundation for working with dreams.

Jung went further than Freud by asserting that the unconscious reflects a higher wisdom within us. He, too, believed that the unconscious is revealed through dreams.

I believe that we accumulate the higher wisdom that Jung spoke of partially through our life experiences. These experiences have taught us important truths, but our conscious minds may not wish to accept them. For instance, these truths could entail seeing things about ourselves or others that we do not wish to acknowledge. Or they could direct us to give up a person, thing, or belief that we are not yet ready to relinquish. The dream is a message from the unconscious that says, in essence, "I have something to tell you and I know you are ready to hear it if you are willing."

Jung believed that dreams reveal more than just the personal unconscious. He invented the concept of a "collective unconscious," containing every thought, feeling, and idea ever conceived in the universe, to cover these experiences. That could explain why Einstein invented the theory of relativity while in a dreamlike state, or why Descartes discovered his theory of rationalism, which affected all of seventeenth-century thinking, through a series of lucid dreams.

There is nothing more powerful than a dream to tell us the truth about our inner condition—no psychiatrist, medical doctor, astrologist, psychic, or sage can offer more pertinent insights. Dreams are created by our unconscious, which knows more about us than any other person, no matter how wise he or she appears to be. In order to gain that wisdom, however, we must involve ourselves with our dreams—the answers will then come to us. This book offers readers who are willing to look inward a variety of methods to unravel their dreams and make them catalysts for transformation in their lives.

The people whose stories appear on these pages listened to their dreams and were willing to courageously leap into the feelings that could release the messages of their dreams. Thanks to their effort and commitment, their lives shifted in dramatic ways. No longer stuck, they were flooded with a rush of new ideas and new ways of looking at their lives and at the world. They sometimes received messages from their waking lives that were related to their dreams—in the form of signs and new directions, all possible and within reach.

These people shared a common determination to discover what prevented them from living the lives they desired. Some of them were extraordinarily gifted, but believed that either some inner flaw or fate had blocked them from realizing their full potential in the world. Some of them were HIV-positive or had AIDS. Their task was to live with—and in spite of—an illness that is unjust, horrific, and fatal. The stories that follow were gathered primarily from my clinical practice.

I have named the chapters after the transformative dreams that caused the changes. Some of the dreamers had already done the difficult preliminary groundwork of dealing with related problems before experiencing their big dreams. Others were still working through their problems when their dreams occurred. Many had to enter their feelings or act out their dream before the message became apparent. Others received their transformative messages in an easy-to-understand, no-interpretation-needed format. One dreamer, an AIDS patient, came to a profound reckoning with the meaning of his life two days before he died, thanks to a clearly spelled out message. In all cases, the dreamers were willing to make the journey through unexplored territory to reach the place where real change could occur. (I have disguised the identities of the participants, while keeping the tenor and flavor of their lives intact.)

In addition to containing the forbidden wishes that Freud said are hidden in the images, symbols, and stories, in my opinion dreams also conceal those feelings the dreamer deems too painful to view. The dreamer may not want to know certain realities, because he fears he can't cope with them. That same dreamer may march through his waking life in a perpetual state of sleep, refusing to experience truths that could be upsetting or could disrupt the balance in his comfortable but unfulfilling life. We are all guilty of this to some degree, albeit unwittingly.

Many dreamworkers *analyze* a dream to expose the dream's message. In my experience, intellectual understanding by itself will not produce a transformation. *In fact, insights usually occur after the dreamer fully experiences the feelings in the dream.* Often a dream's images, symbols, and stories are so bizarre that the dreamer hasn't a clue about the dream's meaning. The dream has succeeded in disguising the message to the point of blotting out the dreamer's true feelings. When the dreamer becomes aware of some of the feelings in the dream, he can use these feelings as a starting point to work on the dream. If the dreamer was already completely in touch with all his feelings, there would be no dream because there would be nothing to conceal behind symbols. It's the dreamwork that follows in the waking state that leads to both the feelings and subsequent transformation. When you awaken from a dream with anxiety, that anxiety is a sure sign that strong feelings are being repressed. My approach focuses on helping the dreamer discover and experience the feelings contained within the dream. All the exercises in this book, either directly or indirectly, aim for that goal.

Sometimes a dreamer does not need my help. She may be so haunted by a particular dream, so close to the message and so desirous of discovering what it is, that she instinctively finds her own way back into the dream and unravels its message. Such was the case of Marcy and her dream, *The Monster in the Closet.* Marcy reentered her dream the day after it occurred, in a therapy group, and allowed herself to experience all the feelings of the dream. This led to an extraordinary change in her. In that chapter, I present an exercise that is based on the method used by Marcy. It enables you to release the deep feelings of your dreams, which can then lead to change and healing.

As noted before, other approaches may help the dreamer discover the meaning of the dream, but significant change usually occurs only when feelings are released. Occasionally the right interpretation from a therapist, or the recollection of a significant memory by the dreamer, may lead to the feelings underneath the repression. I sometimes use analytic techniques during the preliminary dreamwork stages to help dreamers deal with their defenses against feelings that may arouse too much anguish or get out of control. Sometimes free association brings forth a memory, and the memory itself may contain feelings similar to those in the dream. I then help the dreamer to experience those feelings if he is unable to do so spontaneously. Dreamwork is a process of interchange between patient and therapist. It is truly an interactive process.

One of therapy's prime accomplishments is in helping patients deal with their anger. And rare, if not nonexistent, is the person who does not have difficulty with this emotion. Adults tend to carry with them all the unresolved baggage of childhood. They continue to deal with their emotions, and not just their anger, in the same defensive way they did during childhood in order to survive. The exercises I use will help you reach your buried feelings. The exercises will make you aware of unexamined aspects of yourself as well as increase your sensitivity to your own intuitive nature. The very act of remembering dreams and then working with them is, in itself, an exercise in intuition.

You may wonder what kind of transformation you can expect. This depends upon you, your life story, and your goals. I can only attest that others have experienced a new purpose in life, new careers, an ability to overcome obstacles to relationships, a new sense of self-worth, wholeness, acceptance of self, fearlessness, and joy—all due to their transformative dreams.

I suggest you keep a dream journal and title each dream. The title should be based upon the key action or key symbol in the dream. The title is the first clue to the meaning of the dream. When you write down the symbols of your dream, permit yourself to feel your emotional reaction to these animate and inanimate objects. What feelings do they arouse? Your personal feelings about these symbols are the best clue to their meanings.

You needn't use a dream dictionary, although the definitions I provide in the book can be helpful in a way I will explain shortly. But first and foremost, let your intuition and feelings be your guide.

If you glance at the titles I have provided for the chapters in this book, you'll understand how they offer clues to the dream's meaning. The first chapter, for example, is entitled "The Token Dispenser." What comes to your mind when you think "token dispenser?" A token dispenser is someone who gives passage. The token dispenser exchanges money for enablement or power, and therefore is an important figure—an alchemist, if you will.

Examine the title of the eleventh chapter and dream: "Crashing Through the Waves." This suggests an action of confrontation, a battle with the obstacles that stand in one's way. Waves suggest something overpowering, deep, and primal, part of nature and the universe.

By studying a dream's title, you will begin to understand the meaning of symbols. You are also encouraged to pay attention to the other symbols in the dream as well. I list each important symbol in **bold** letters so that it catches your eye when you flip through the book. I then list meanings for these symbols stemming from my own extensive work with dreams and from what I've learned from other therapists and dreamworkers. For example, the symbol **doll** will be followed by definitions such as "toy," "dead child," "sexual object," etc. An index at the back of the book will enable you to quickly look up the meanings of the symbols in your dreams. Although these definitions are not as precise as the ones you discover for yourself, they can offer a clue to the dream's meaning. Dreams have many levels of meaning, and a universal symbol definition can trigger personal associations as well. These dream definitions will assist you in developing your own symbol vocabulary.

Some dreamers became sensitized, through their dreams, to signs and occurrences in waking reality that led them in new directions in their lives. I worked directly with others to help them release the feelings contained within their dream. Having practiced twenty years as a psychotherapist and dream specialist, I follow my intuition and hunches. Since the meaning must ultimately be discovered by the dreamer, my task is to help the dreamer navigate to that place. My knowledge of the dreamer from our previous work together provides further clues to the direction to follow. Sometimes I go with the feelings the dreamer brings into the session; other times I prompt the dreamer to explore the symbol itself so that the meaning may burst out of its symbolic covering.

One last word. The meaning of the dream may pop up unexpectedly. It doesn't always happen when you doggedly pursue it. The meaning is more likely to come to you when you are relaxed, even tired, off-guard, in touch with your feelings. An intellectual probing may only push the dream's meaning further into obscurity.

This is more than just a book about dreams, though it does teach you the techniques that can turn your dreams into solutions to life's problems. It is also a guide to unveiling your feelings, so that your life can become richer and more meaningful.

ONE

The Token Dispenser

The dreamer, whom I shall call Mark, was an unusually articulate, reflective, and intelligent man. He came to therapy because he was having severe panic attacks, which started shortly after he broke up with the woman he loved. While he was having them, he thought that he actually might hurt someone. Mark was currently working as a cop in a city precinct, and often described the dangerous situations he encountered on a daily basis. He was fearless when it came to doing his job and never retreated from danger, even when his life was at risk. However, away from the job, he felt that his life had lost its meaning. Increasingly morose and alienated, he often remained detached and distant during our therapy sessions. Mark had this dream toward the end of his first year of therapy. He brushed it off as only a "snippet" of a dream, but I encouraged him to tell it to me anyway.

DREAM: *I go down into the subway to the token booth. Sitting in the booth is an older man for whom I have great admiration. He is a precinct captain in the police force. I give him ten dollars, and he asks me, with a mischievous wink, if I'd like a thousand tokens. I reply, "I'll just take four." I take the tokens and leave.*

Mark had no inkling as to what this dream meant. We had spent months trying to understand and explain his terrors, but the panic attacks, which kept him vigilant and anxious, persisted. He had many insights during the therapy, but his feelings did not change. Finally, in desperation, he asked his medical doctor to prescribe an antianxiety drug. The therapy continued, although with noticeably less enthusiasm on his part. He happily extolled the virtues of the drug and insisted he felt much better. During one session, he told me he was taking off the next week to go hiking. Later in the session, he casually told me the dream reported above.

Before proceeding with the dream, let me fill you in on some pertinent data about this patient. It will then make sense to you why this dream, which at first glance seemed undramatic, became a turning point in Mark's life once we discovered its meaning.

Mark came from an accomplished family. His father was a doctor and his mother was president of a local woman's group and a fund-raiser for a new maternity wing at the hospital where her husband was affiliated. They were enormously disappointed when their brilliant son decided to join the police force. Mark made his choice partly out of defiance toward his father and partly out of an inner compulsion to overcome his fears. Doing the very thing one is afraid of is an unconscious defense mechanism called "reaction formation" in psychological parlance.

Why had he needed to create this defense? Mark described himself as an only child who was extraordinarily happy during the first eight years of his life. He portrayed this period as "familial bliss," and believed those years gave him the strength to cope with what followed. Everything changed when his adopted brother Aaron entered the picture, and the family. Aaron was

actually his first cousin, his father's sister's son. Both of
his parents were killed in an automobile accident where
he was the only survivor. Aaron was eight years old, the
same age as my patient, at the time of adoption. He was
an angry, resentful, and distrustful boy. Before the
accident, his alcoholic father would beat him while
drunk. Aaron's mother was never present to stop the
abuse, or if she was, she pretended not to notice. She
worked long hours to keep the family together, because
her husband's alcoholism prevented him from holding a
job. She often left the apartment early in the morning,
while Aaron was still sleeping, and by the time he returned home from school, she had gone to bed. She was
constantly depressed and complained of fatigue and
weakness. Aaron was left on his own. He had to make
his own meals and get ready for school by himself.
Lonely and abandoned, he started getting into trouble.

The trouble did not stop when Aaron joined his new
family. At first, Mark's parents tried to understand Aaron's behavior and talk to him about it. But all their
understanding and advice was to no avail. Aaron continued to misbehave. His teachers reported that he
daydreamed during class, didn't do his homework, and
frequently skipped school. He was picked up several
times for stealing food and toys from neighborhood
stores. Soon Mark's father's patience gave way to anger
and then violence. He beat Aaron mercilessly with a
strap, but the boy defiantly refused to cry. Instead, the
beatings led to more destructive forms of acting out.
He'd get into fights with other kids and once tried to
throw a classmate out the window. Mark's parents, who
were prominent in the community, felt publicly humiliated by Aaron's behavior. As the punishments grew
more severe, the tension in the family increased. The

beatings became so harsh, in fact, that my patient pleaded with his father to hit him instead of Aaron.

Where was Aaron's adoptive mother at this time? She was absent, just like Aaron's birth mother. Though deeply conflicted over what her husband was doing, she was too intimidated by him to interfere. She also felt she would be a disloyal wife if she disagreed with him. This, coupled with her ambivalent feelings toward Aaron, enabled the beatings to continue. Mark's mother had adopted this boy out of goodwill, but her plan didn't turn out the way she had envisioned it. She dissociated herself from what was happening by turning her back on the family, and poured herself even more zealously than before into her community activities. As a result, Mark was also neglected.

Mark tried to compensate for his troubled brother by going out of his way to be good, in the hopes that this would hold the family together. At the same time, he developed terrible feelings of guilt for being the good child. Mark didn't understand how his father could change from a loving, amiable dad into this raging, uncontrollable wild man. His father's behavior frightened him, and he was terrified of becoming the next victim. He grieved over the emotional loss of his two loving parents. Unbeknownst to him at the time, his parents had their own marital problems and Aaron's adoption only exacerbated their difficulties.

Despite his fear, Mark still cherished his father. Soon his father began staying away from home for several nights at a time. My patient listened for him anxiously every evening, afraid that if he stopped coming home altogether the burden of the family would fall on him, now a nine-year-old boy. He heard his mother crying and didn't know what to do, so he did the only thing he could. He tried his best to be the most helpful, most studious, most perfect boy in the world, both to comfort his mother and to get his father to come back home. It didn't work. Eventually his parents separated and then divorced. When his father moved out of the house, Mark realized that all his attempts to be the good son had failed to keep the family together. His belief in everything collapsed. He became cynical and hid his feelings from everyone. Although he was popular with his classmates, he never allowed anyone to become too close.

Mark discovered early on that he had an excellent ear for music. He loved the piano and started taking lessons when he was five years old. He continued to play the piano, despite the turmoil in the house. Eventually he became an accomplished musician. By the time Mark was in high school, he had also learned the violin and clarinet and taught himself to compose and orchestrate music. His dream was to go to a music school so that he could pursue a career in music.

It never occurred to Mark that his father would not pay for his education, since he could easily afford it. My patient still believed that his father loved him and would eventually return to being the loving father of his early years. By this time his father had resumed his medical practice in another part of town. Just before his high school graduation, Mark visited his father to break the good news that he had been accepted at music school. His father showed no interest. He asked his father to pay for school anyhow, and his father said no. Mark begged him, but his father wouldn't yield. The young man was heartbroken. He couldn't believe that his father would betray him like that and questioned whether his father ever loved him. The event marked the beginning of his dissociation from his feelings toward his father. He lost all faith in his father, whom he had tried to forgive in spite of his many betrayals. Mark cried violently, and it was the last time he ever cried. Eventually he abandoned his love of music and joined the police force.

Returning to the dream, I asked Mark to describe the precinct captain sitting in the token booth. As he listed the man's physical characteristics—muscular, wiry, thick white hair—he remembered that he had had an encounter with him the day before the dream. Mark admired the precinct captain and hoped to emulate him one day. He said he was both brilliant and tough, skillfully running the department while always maintaining his integrity, despite the unrelenting pressure. The precinct captain noticed Mark walking through the cafeteria that day and motioned him over to the table where he was having lunch with two of his assistants. He seemed to have a special liking for Mark, who had already attracted the favorable attention of some of his other superiors. My patient joined the precinct captain at his table but felt uncomfortable. Within a few minutes he felt stirrings of panic, which he quickly quelled with his medication.

During the ensuing therapy, it became apparent to both of us that there was an unmistakable connection between the panic attacks and his fear of separation and abandonment. The panic also appeared when he was in the presence of a superior he admired.

As the patient spoke affectionately about this precinct captain, telling me what he knew of his life, it occurred to me that the man in the dream was a representation of his good father. I kept this information to myself until I found the right moment, when Mark was emotionally ready, to ask him about it. I took Mark step-by-step through the dream.

"You are walking through a subway. What does that

feel like?" I asked him. He said he felt he was going underground, below the surface. This suggested to me that the subway was a metaphor for Mark's unconscious feelings. Dreams are filled with symbols and metaphors, which comprise the language of the unconscious. These symbols and metaphors express complicated thoughts, ideas, and feelings in a succinct and vivid fashion.

Although it's helpful for the therapist to be aware of the meanings of symbols, transformation only occurs when the patient experiences the feelings contained within the symbols. It is far better for the patient to say what the symbols mean than for the therapist to supply the meaning. A therapist should only mention an interpretation if she is absolutely certain she is on the same wavelength as the patient.

In this dream, the patient went to a token booth. To me this represented a place where money is exchanged for power, where a token can open locked doors and give passageway through turnstiles, which are barriers to getting from one place to another. I kept this information to myself. It was helpful to know that the token dispenser was an important person to the dreamer. It was both Mark's feelings for the precinct captain and the captain's age that suggested to me he was a symbol for Mark's father. I knew that Mark felt his father was inaccessible. The token booth, which surrounded the token dispenser and separated him from Mark, symbolized how unavailable the father was.

It is not unusual for money to change hands between father and son. A token dispenser changes money into energy and functionality. When the dreamer gave the token clerk a ten-dollar bill, the symbolic father affectionately winked and said, "Would you like a thousand tokens?" meaning "I'm happy to give you a hundred times more than you're asking for. In other words, I am happy and willing to give you unconditional love." (His father, as you may recall, gave him no money, no love, and no support when he asked for it.) The paternal love offered in this dream was sorely lacking in the patient's waking reality, and the dream indicated Mark's fervent longing for it. That was his unconscious wish.

When the dreamer was offered his father's unconditional love, which he wanted more than anything in the world, he stoically refused it by saying he would take four tokens. I asked Mark what tokens meant to him, and he answered, "Proof." It is significant that four tokens is *less* than he deserved for his ten dollars. The patient literally shortchanged himself in his dream. That is what people often do when they haven't gotten the love they're entitled to. They continue to act out that early deprivation in other ways. They are not able to accept love because they never got it as children, and to admit the need now would be humiliating. Unconsciously they believe they got what they deserved, even though what they got was nothing. They are convinced they do not deserve more. As you may recall, it was after my patient broke up with his girlfriend that his panic attacks began. Although he rationalized his separation from her by telling himself "She's not right for me, she's not smart enough," and so on, his unconscious was really protecting him from feeling the early longing for love (directed toward his father) that led to such rejection and pain. The pain was so unbearable that the patient unwittingly chose to block off his feelings rather than chance reexperiencing the denial of love.

My patient was unwilling to feel his deep longing for his father's love because that meant opening himself up to all the anguish he had experienced, and then buried, as a child. The sting of disappointment, the ache of unmet needs, the torment of rejection, and the agony of feeling that his father did not love him threatened to overwhelm him. Mark's first visible blow came when his father delivered the news that he wouldn't pay his tuition at music school. Mark, who had always been religious, lost his faith in God. (Was this God, the father, or Father, the god?) He confided that the loss of his religious faith precipitated the breakup with his girlfriend, which led to his first panic attack. One of his complaints when he entered therapy was that his life had lost its meaning. Mark had had a multitude of losses over a short span of time—he'd lost a career in music, his father, a belief in God, and his girlfriend.

Going back to the dream again, I asked Mark why he shortchanged himself in the dream. He looked at me questioningly. "You deserved eight tokens for your ten dollars," I said, "but when the token dispenser offered you a thousand, you only asked for four, which is half the amount you were entitled to. Did someone teach you that you couldn't have what you wanted, what you deserved?" "My father," Mark answered numbly. Then all his emotions welled up inside of him—his longing for love, his feelings of abandonment, and his deep, unabiding sadness. Mark was afraid to tell his father that he needed him and loved him.

Dreams are able to give us all the things we seem unable to get in waking life. Freud claimed that all dreams were wishes. I do not agree that "all" dreams are such, but some certainly are, and this one clearly is. Mark desperately wished for his father's love, but when he created a symbolic father in his dream (the precinct captain) who was willing to give him that love (a thousand tokens), he had to refuse it. The pain of acknowledging that unfulfilled need was too great. But that hurt was exactly what he needed to feel in order to regain contact with his emotions and have meaning in his life.

Sometimes a symptom becomes as painful as the very thing it tries to hide, although in a different way. Mark's panic attacks—his symptom—were so unbearable he feared he might pass out. He never knew when the next panic attack would strike, so he lived in constant fear. However, once a person accepts and actually feels the underlying cause behind the symptom, the symptom disintegrates.

The symptom occurred in the first place because the patient, as a child, did not have a sufficient structural development to withstand the shocks and hurts of his life. Nor did he have anyone with whom he could share his concerns. During childhood, it's up to adults (a loving mother, father, grandparent, etc.) to provide safety and strength for the child. If the adult is not available, the child creates his own survival tactics—ways to protect himself so that he can survive in childhood. Unfortunately, these survival tactics usually leave him weak and empty inside, without a solid core of inner strength. When he becomes an adult, he is still fixated at that same emotional stage of childhood because the trauma has prevented him from developing. Thus, when he encounters a situation that is similar to the traumatic one, those repressed memories and feelings are revived. As an adult, though, he has the ability to confront and experience those buried childhood feelings, and, in the process, become whole again.

During our ensuing therapy sessions, things that had been incomprehensible before now began to make sense to my patient. For example, why did he chose a career that made him risk his life? There were many reasons. As a child with an out-of-control father and absent mother, he had a wish for law and order in the house. He wanted someone to protect this adopted brother, a destructive but still vulnerable child. And as a boy,

Mark wanted to stand up to his father but was too frightened. Joining the police force was a way to become someone powerful, someone who could stop violence.

Another contributing factor was the reaction formation I mentioned earlier. Mark unconsciously chose to deny the fear caused by his violent childhood by taking an action that was contrary to that fear. He picked a job that forced him to confront cruelty, violence, and inhumanity—situations reminiscent of his early childhood—every day. His panic attacks came partly from repressing his feelings of repulsion and fear.

Mark also believed that he had to save others. That was his way of expiating the guilt he felt over seeing his adopted brother beaten. He wondered why Aaron was punished and he wasn't. In his unconscious mind, he transformed the precinct captain, whom he so greatly admired, into an idealized father—whose love he hoped to win by his brave and caring actions. As a child he had tried, unsuccessfully, to lure his father back to the family in the same manner.

One of the biggest changes that occurred after Mark experienced the underlying feelings of his dream was the dimunition of his panic attacks. Instead of feeling panic, he felt rage. He had dreams in which he screamed at his father. In one nightmare—a childhood scene with snow on the ground—he followed his father with a shovel and tried to beat him senseless, all the while yelling that he wanted to beat the snow out of him. The snow, of course, represented his father's coldness. Before these dreams, Mark was incapable of expressing anger toward anyone. As we worked on each subsequent dream, Mark realized not only that his father had failed him, but also how angry and disappointed this made him. He felt heartbreak and grief over his father's desertion.

Eventually he faced the fact that the father whom he idealized was nothing more than a coward who always ran away from his feelings. This was an empowering realization, because it freed Mark from the despair of waiting for his father's love and wishing things were different. Instead, he accepted that he would never get what he wanted from his family because they were incapable of giving what he needed. As Mark recaptured his own buried emotions, his self-worth grew in leaps and bounds.

He was promoted at his job and rewarded with better assignments. He took those rewards in stride—rather than viewing them as undeserved challenges he was bound to bungle. He also made the decision to stop running from one woman to the next, and instead chose to deal with the uncomfortable feelings that got stirred up during intimacy.

Incidentally, Mark went off his antianxiety drug shortly after we worked on his dream. His life is almost completely free of panic now and is much more fulfilling. When the anxiety does appear, it is more manageable. He knows he must continue to work through his insights. He claims that he now has a wonderful and pervasive sense of hope and goodness he lacked before.

I sometimes wonder what might have happened if Mark's dream had been either ignored or misinterpreted. No one can say for sure, but I'm inclined to think that he would have remained stuck with his fear, his longing, and his failed relationships. Of course, one dream cannot solve an entire trauma without preliminary groundwork. This dream appeared only after the soil had been tilled and the dreamer was ready and could listen to the message. Sometimes, however, the message may be so disturbing that it takes considerable effort and patience to work through the terror and pain that may accompany the insight.

Make note of some of the symbols in Mark's dream, for they may help you understand your own dreams. The meanings listed below are only possibilities; the real definitions must come from your own dreamwork.

Symbols for Your Dream Dictionary:

Subway: Underground; underneath; below the surface; unconscious mind.

Token booth: Where money transactions take place; enclosed, protected space.

Older man: Father; experienced; wise.

Captain: Leader; person in charge.

Ten dollars: Power (the amount of money must be viewed within the context of the dream).

Tokens: Proof; representations of money.

Exercise: Walk Yourself Through Your Dream, Scene by Scene, Symbol by Symbol

You can apply this technique with any dream. Approach each symbol and action of your dream in the order in which it occurs. Let yourself experience the feelings behind the symbols and the actions. Here are some questions you might ask yourself that will implement the process:

1. What is the feeling in the dream?
2. Are the dream characters anyone I know?
3. What do they represent to me? (Authority? Sexual attraction? Feelings of affection, anger, disdain, admiration, etc.? Are the dream characters older/ younger than I am?)
4. What feelings are awakened in me by the action(s) in the dream?

After all these questions are answered, go on to Question Five.

5. Am I having any nagging preoccupations or problems in my life now?
6. Last and most important, am I able to *feel* the message of my dream?

I used this exercise in one of my dream workshops. One of the participants had an important insight. She had had a dream in which she took her tiger-striped cat to the veterinarian. As the vet was examining the cat, the woman noticed that the stripes on the cat were all different colors; it looked just like an expensive Italian sweater she owned. The vet was astonished; he admired the cat, saying he'd never seen one like that before.

The woman asked herself each of the above questions and came up with the following answers: (1) She was delighted that her cat was special and even magical, because no cat like that actually exists. (2) She knew both the vet and the cat in waking life. (3) She saw the vet as an authority figure, a caregiver and healer who knew more about cats than she did. (4) She felt pride and happiness.

From answering these questions, the dreamer realized that something she owned (her cat) was unusual and special and won admiration from a revered person. She felt wonderful about this. She then went on to Question Five—and thought about something that was troubling her. She felt that her supervisor at work was ignoring her. She believed it was because he found her work ordinary. The dream fulfilled her wish to be recognized as special. This dream brought up her suppressed feelings of hurt regarding this situation. By letting herself give in completely to the hurt feelings, she remembered how her father never seemed happy to see her; he treated her off-handedly as a child. She realized that the feeling of not being special was one she unconsciously carried around with her in her life, and perhaps had little to do with how others treated her.

Try the exercise with one of your dreams.

TWO

The Wailing Wall

While traveling through Israel, a patient whom I'll call Peggy felt alone and isolated from the others in her tour group. This was nothing new, for she had felt like an outsider all her life. Although she graduated with honors from medical school and was awarded a research fellowship in endocrinology, the young doctor never felt comfortable in social situations. On this trip, she tried to make friendly overtures, but she was convinced nobody liked her. She concluded there must be something wrong with her. Her hurt escalated to panic when she did a mental inventory of all her shortcomings.

Peggy had tried to overcome her social fears by continually forcing herself to join groups. The people she traveled with in Israel were a good deal older than she, which compounded her isolation. In addition, most of them were accompanied by husbands, wives, lovers, and friends, while she was traveling alone. The few people who were also traveling by themselves had made alliances with each other or other members of the group. That dreaded, and familiar, feeling of being left out became so overwhelming that she began counting the days till the trip would end. Once again excluded, Peggy was barraged by a flood of vivid, painful memories of similar situations.

Peggy blamed herself for her current predicament. It seemed that nothing she had done to alleviate these feelings—none of her therapy with me, none of the workshops she'd taken—had worked. This was one of her journal entries from the trip:

I feel the futility of everything I've done—the years of therapy, the forcing myself to join groups. Nothing erases the feeling that I am separate, that I have written myself out of the universe. I sit at a table eating lunch with other people, unable to relate to them, and am overcome by my feelings of panic, hopelessness, and even doom. I try to keep a pleasant expression on my face, so as not to betray my real feelings. I struggle to keep in my tears. I don't want anyone to notice my pain.

When lunch breaks we all pile onto the bus to go to the Old City. This action alleviates some of the panic of feeling separate and lost. When we arrive at the Western Gate, I walk by myself to the Wailing Wall to join the rest of the group. As I stand in front of the Wall with the others, I notice cracks where people have inserted written prayers. Although I am not religious, I close my eyes and wait for a prayer to come to me. Suddenly the word "Help" shouts from somewhere inside. I know it has come from a deep place within me. My whole being is thrust into this prayer.

Later that night I have a dream—a dream that ultimately changed my life, for it was the answer to my prayer.

DREAM: *I go to a therapy group that my therapist recommended. I feel tuned out, in my own world, not part of what is happening. I think I use this spaciness to protect myself from the anxiety of being with people I do not know. I don't think I will remain in the group because everyone looks at least a generation older than me. I sense, however, a comfortable informality in the way the therapist handles the group. During the break, I tell him privately that I don't want to stay in the group. He convinces me to stick it out till the end of the session. Even though I agree to finish the session, I'm sure I'll never come back to the group again.*

I'm outside and a woman smiles at me through a glass terrace door. I don't return the smile. After all, this is a place to be myself, and if I don't feel like smiling then I won't. When I come back inside I notice she is only about three feet high, and is now standing in a corner with her back to everyone. I have hurt her feelings. I decide to talk to her, and she becomes the reason I stay in the group. I overhear someone say the leader is a genius. I notice everyone looks different. They are not the same group of people as before; they all have some kind of malady or imperfection. I feel at home here, that I can connect with these people. I decide to be very honest about myself with this group.

Peggy was ecstatic after having this dream. She described the feeling as "one of relief, satisfaction, a deep sense of connection, a reason for being, and an acceptance of myself." She knew that this dream had told her something profound about herself, but wasn't sure what it was. She focused on the three-foot-high woman and continued thinking about her until something finally clicked. She had hurt this woman's feelings by not acknowledging her. She's just like me, Peggy thought. I would have felt the same way.

The woman's face was very vivid in her mind—it was sensitive, intelligent, and wise. Peggy realized that this woman was her mirror image, for she had seen her in the dream through a glass patio door (like a mirror). This mirror gave her the distance to look at herself as if she was a separate person.

But why was the woman only three feet tall? she wondered; Peggy herself was five feet eight. It seemed as if this woman had not grown up in one sense, for her face was mature but her body was not. Perhaps the woman had never recovered from some early hurt, Peggy reflected. Or perhaps the size of the woman depicted the parts of herself that felt small and crippled. Peggy felt compassion for this small woman. She admired the sensitivity and intelligence in her face and respected the pain that this woman had endured. The tiny woman was struggling to be big. She was attempting to overcome her hurts, but still felt overwhelmed by them. After the dream, Peggy decided it was futile to try to pretend to be someone other than who she was. She felt her previous efforts to be accepted by the tour group were ugly gyrations of twisting into attitudes and postures that covered up her true self. She concluded that these protections, although subtle, must have been offputting to others. Every time she thought of the tiny woman in her dream, she got a greater sense of who she was. For the first time, Peggy felt self-acceptance.

The next day, when she greeted her fellow travelers, Peggy immediately noticed that something had changed. Her companions were unusually responsive to her and seemed to genuinely like her. She didn't feel her usual discomfort. Her exchanges with them were effortless and natural. She realized that the change was due to her new acceptance of herself. She no longer gave them mixed messages, and she had dropped the defenses that had probably confused them. She felt connected to both herself and to them. No longer an outsider, Peggy was able to enjoy both the people in her tour group and the trip itself.

Peggy then examined the dream for the other truths it seemed to contain. She discovered that all she had to do to connect with others was accept herself. Until she had this dream, she lacked an inner sense of who she really was. The dream woman gave her an image with which she could identify. But Peggy recognized another message in the dream as well: She could not fully accept herself without also accepting the parts of herself that felt damaged. In the past, Peggy had hoped that she would gain other people's love and respect by becoming a physician. But despite having received outer recognition for both her status and accomplishments as a doctor, her feelings about herself hadn't changed. The dream showed her she was still carrying around the psychological injuries of her childhood.

Most of us unwittingly believe that other people see us the way we *unconsciously* view ourselves, and Peggy was no exception. Unconsciously she saw herself as crippled—and tried to hide her defects and the accompanying shame. She was convinced that people would reject her because of these flaws—and could only feel comfortable (in the dream) with others who were also damaged (the new therapy group). The original therapy group in the dream represented the group of people she was traveling with in Israel. It was too painful for her, both in waking and dreaming life, to stay with this group, so she spaced out with them in the dream the same way she unknowingly did in waking life. This was her way of protecting herself. Though she longed to be herself, she was only willing to risk that with people whom she believed were like her: damaged.

Until Peggy could *feel* the ways in which she was crippled, she couldn't come to terms with herself. The dream showed her what so many people wish to discover—her real identity. Once Peggy recognized that the woman in the dream was herself, she made a concerted effort to experience herself as that woman, to feel her smallness and her hurt. She had a visceral reaction. "Okay," she concluded, "this is who I am. I don't intend to hide it any longer."

But Peggy also had a great need to be herself with other people and still be accepted by them. In the dream, the people she felt comfortable with were people like herself, marred and imperfect. This insight helped her to see how she separated herself from others by assuming that others were perfect. Perfect people, she reasoned, would not accept her and her flaws. She had unconsciously divided the world into the damaged and the undamaged, and put herself in the first group.

Where did her feelings of being damaged come from? she wondered. Was it her susceptibility to being easily hurt (like the woman in the dream), or did the hurt feelings result from feeling damaged? These were some of the questions the dream posed for her.

As far back as she could remember, Peggy's mother had derided her for being overly sensitive. When her mother was late picking her up from school she never apologized, just acted rushed and impatient. It was clear her *mother* was *in*sensitive, because she ignored Peggy. Peggy only reacted as any child might. Once when Peggy was a small child, her mother left her on the beach. She gathered up Peggy's older brothers and sister but forgot Peggy. It was not surprising that Peggy felt unimportant to her mother. Many similar memories came back to Peggy.

During high school, Peggy felt isolated because she was too shy to accept invitations to sororities and clubs. A few years later, Peggy learned that her high school had banned sororities; apparently others had also felt excluded. Peggy relived all the times she went away for college weekends. Whether or not she was with a date, the same scenario always took place. She went to all the parties and events, and gradually became increasingly withdrawn. She dreaded speaking in front of others, for fear that everything she said would sound wrong. She grew more silent, self-conscious, and depressed by the minute. Her date, if she had one, never knew what was wrong. Peggy felt like a failure. What she feared the most became a self-fulfilling prophecy.

Reevaluating these memories helped Peggy recognize she was not to blame for her shyness and insecurity. Her mother's excessive criticism and neglect had damaged Peggy's sense of self-worth.

One of the advantages of experiencing pain (rather than running away from it) is that the pain brings up the problem that needs to be solved. Like a magnet, it draws similar experiences from the past that contain the origins of the pain. Once the person looks at the original cause of the pain, he or she can reexperience the feelings that were subsequently buried and thus be free of them.

Dreams deal with pain by disguising it. They are metaphoric messages that contain unexpressed feelings within the symbols. Sometimes the dreamer unlocks the message in a dream by simply delving deeper into the feelings she is already experiencing. Let us say the dreamer is feeling sad that day. While she allows the feeling to come up, a fragment of her dream suddenly comes to mind and she now knows immediately what it means. The dream may then give her even more information about the pain she is experiencing and take her back to an earlier memory where the pain originated. The feeling has unraveled the dream, and the dream clarifies the feeling. Once we are willing to see what our dreams mean, we can understand what is behind our pain. We can face the truths that will free us and allow us to move forward in our lives. That's why looking at our dreams at times of crisis can be both healing and informative. The feeling—whether it be hurt, anger, resentment, or fear—is the magnetic force, collecting past memories that reflect the person's repeated attempts to deal with the original trauma.

When a person is able to unlock or surrender to the *whole* feeling, healing can finally take place. People tend to repeat the same tragic or unrewarding experiences again and again, until they eventually cope with the underlying problem. They usually do not know the source of their terrible feelings and may attribute them to something irrelevant. But the deep expression of the feelings usually leads to the missing information.

Until someone is ready to accept that there is a problem, he or she usually can't be helped. Perhaps that is the function of pain, to tease the problem out into the open and push the person over the threshold of his or her defense. Only then does the alcoholic, who has been denying his drinking problem, admit he is an alcoholic; or the severely ill person, who has been avoiding the doctor, seek one out; or the unloved child, who insists her parents love her, face the devastating truth. Peggy's size in the dream, only three feet high, suggests that her problems originated in childhood.

Another fascinating thing about Peggy's dream is that help appeared only after she asked for it. Up until then she felt the pain without understanding what caused it. But when she prayed for help at the Western (Wailing) Wall, she received a dream that night that answered her prayer. Peggy saw religious overtones in her experience. Being in Israel got her in touch with her Jewish identity, something she rarely thought about. She felt her ancient heritage, especially at the Wailing Wall, and for the first time in her life thought about the lives of her grandparents and great-grandparents. When she visited the Holocaust Museum, she marveled at her grandparents' bravery in leaving their homeland to risk a life on unfamiliar land. If they had remained in their native country, they might have been killed by the Nazis and she would never have been born.

The dream proved that pain can be a catalyst for change. But perhaps pain may not suffice. Perhaps, as I suggested earlier, there must also be some kind of surrender, a willingness to drop one's defenses or ego. Unfortunately, a conscious choice to do that may not be enough. In therapy, change occurs most rapidly when the patient stops resisting the process. Patients bring their bodies to therapy but often oppose the help that is offered. They may unconsciously erect the deeply embedded patterns that cause so much turmoil when they sense danger. The person appears determined to maintain those patterns, no matter how painful they are, because at least they are familiar. Nothing is scarier than the unknown.

Peggy's transformation did not come from discovering her defects, as illustrated in the dream, but rather from seeing herself as she truly was. She stopped trying to figure out what was wrong with her—a fruitless lifelong pursuit that originated from her feelings of not being loved as a child. Peggy decided to pursue a course of action that was suggested in her dream—joining a therapy group where she would feel safe to talk about her shameful feelings of being emotionally crippled. The dream brought out her yearning to stop hiding her pain from others and start revealing herself just as she was. When she returned from Israel, she asked me to recommend a therapy group for her, which I did.

It was no accident that Peggy had dreamed of a therapy group. Somewhere inside her she knew that having people listen to her would be an important part of her healing process. It would be an affirmation of her new voice; the group would be able to mirror her the way her mother never did. After years of stifling herself, what Peggy longed for the most was to be heard. Only then could she truly feel loved.

Symbols for Your Dream Dictionary:

Group: Public opinion, which may be at variance with the views of the dreamer.

Glass: Mirror.

Terrace door: Passageway between the inside and the outside, the conscious and the unconscious mind.

Exercise: Ask for What You Didn't Get in Your Dream: Love, Support, Recognition, Forgiveness, etc.

Define this need and then feel it as fully as you can. Simply acknowledging the feelings intellectually will not help you; you must experience the emotion. Write down what it would feel like to be loved by the person you long for in your dream, what it would feel like to be a success in that situation, or whatever it is that you want. What other feelings, memories, associations does expressing this need bring up? Follow those feelings wherever they lead. . . . How do you feel now?

Roger, a middle-aged man, had the following dream:

DREAM: *I'm in the office of a friend's family busi-*
ness. It's located in a very fancy building. I try to re-
member the name of the company, so I can later
boast to my parents about it. The company is a leader
in the field, globally recognized for its achievements.
My father's office is also in this building. Although
he's achieved some degree of success, his company is
decidedly more modest than my friend's internation-
ally known business.

Earlier in the dream I see myself as young (thirty
years old) and handsome, elegantly dressed in an ex-
pensive suit with a Calvin Klein tie. I am sitting
among others at a business seminar. I see myself as
the son my parents would have been proud of. In the
dream I also idealize my parents, and there is the
strong sense of security that comes from being confi-
dent that we appreciate one another. We are a very
successful family.

Roger's sense of his parents' love was strong in this
dream, and he felt a deep sense of loss when he woke
up. His parents had been dead for twenty years, and the
dream story did not accurately depict the way his life
had turned out. Roger decided to do the exercise and
ask his parents for their love and approval. He wrote the
following:

I deeply regret that I did not live up to your expectations. Maybe if I had, we would have been a happy
family. In my dream, status was important. All I ever
wanted to do was be a writer and fulfill myself from
inside. I know I threw aside everything you worked

so hard to achieve, Mom and Dad. I took it all for granted, as if it had no value. The dream tells me that if I had been what you wanted, we all would have been happy.

But I could never see myself as an aggressive, corporate type, ordering people around and earning tons of money. I felt then as I do now—raw, rebellious, unhappy. My achievements were of a different sort. I became a novelist and wrote five books, none of which became bestsellers. I had love affairs but never married and raised a family.

The dream seems to be saying that I would have been surrounded by love and people if I had followed the conventional path. I would have made you proud. Instead I tried to make myself proud, but it didn't get me what I wanted; it didn't bring me love, or friends, or recognition. This dream seems to say that only *your* recognition could have made me happy.

I awoke from this dream feeling your loss so strongly. I have no family support. Perhaps you could never love me for who I was. Perhaps I showed you that I couldn't love you, either. I certainly didn't do what you wanted. Maybe the dream says that I *couldn't* do what you wanted, even though perhaps I wanted to. I think of our family as shipwrecked. Maybe your approval meant much more to me than I ever acknowledged. Maybe I can never find happiness by following my own path.

Is the dream saying that my unconventional path was wrong for me? Even if I had been an obedient son, I would have been lying. The fault does not all lie with me. Does this mean there is no happiness for me? That in order to be loved I have to be someone other than myself? How can I be content if I deny who I am?

How can I ask you to accept me when I don't accept me? Have I accepted only *your* idea of what is satisfactory and proper? Can I only feel self-acceptance if I live up to that standard? But I can't do that now and I couldn't do it before.

Is being angry at you the only way I can accept myself? Is striving for recognition, the recognition I never got from you, my only option? I must stop telling myself I don't want recognition, because that is a lie.

What would make me happy now? In my fantasy, I would have people around me who loved me and often reminded me of it. I would feel that they appreciated me. They'd invite me to their homes and to their parties, and they would not be upset if I wasn't able to accept. My friends would know my problems and concerns, and they would check up on me regularly to make sure that I was okay. They might even try to help me. They would be a substitute for you, the parents I never had.

After writing this, Roger realized why he so frequently felt depressed. It was because he felt that he lacked support. Until now he had not known the cause. He also saw that he didn't do much to get the things, and the *life*, he wanted. The reason for this became clear: He had failed in his first task as a child—to win his parents' love. Therefore he unconsciously believed he was doomed to fail at anything else he undertook. Roger understood that he needed what we all need—love and support in our present lives. He made a concerted effort to acquire that support. Since he enjoyed working on his dreams, his first step was to join a dream group. Although none of us can ever get the parental love that was denied in childhood, Roger discovered that this group was able to give him some of the support and recognition that he so desperately needed.

THREE

The Message on the Blackboard

Twenty-five years ago, Joan Witkowski had the following dream. At the time, she thought it was meaningless, but it ultimately changed her life. All she could remember was the last fragment of the dream. The fragment was:

> DREAM: *I see a blackboard. On it, written in chalk in large white letters, is the following message: "I want to learn massage."*

This fragment of a dream led Joan to finding her life's work and, more importantly to Joan, her spiritual center. It was also during this time that she met her life partner. When this dream occurred, more than twenty-five years ago, Joan was in a transient state. She didn't want her own apartment and preferred just to float. It was important to her not to get too attached to the material world. She worked at a job she didn't like, but it gave her a lot of free time to pursue an acting career and be involved with the theater. It was a carefree, fun time in her life and she enjoyed it thoroughly.

Then she had this dream, while subletting a friend's apartment. She awakened that morning with the image of a sentence written in chalk on a blackboard still fresh in her mind: "I want to learn massage." Joan thought that was very strange because (A) she had never had a massage, and (B) she didn't know anyone who actually had had one, either, except her father, who occasionally mentioned rubdowns when talking about the sports he played as a youth.

This dream occurred in the late sixties, and the two images that came to Joan's mind when she thought of "massage" reflected the times: big Swedish women at a Fifth Avenue salon, and the numerous massage parlors that operated as de facto brothels. Joan thought, Well, that's definitely nothing I'm interested in, and tried to put the dream aside. Yet for some reason the dream stayed with her. She was perplexed by its message because she couldn't understand what massage had to do with her, since it was in no way connected with her life. Joan was determined to be either an actress or an English professor. She was no more interested in being a masseuse than in being a nuclear physicist.

That summer, not long after she had the dream, she had dinner with the director of a play she was in. He was the first person she confided in about this mysterious dream. As it turned out, he had studied at the Esalen Institute. He told Joan, "Some people from Esalen are coming to New York to do a massage and meditation workshop. Why don't you try it?" Joan had always been interested in meditation. She was also curious about Esalen and the whole encounter movement because it was tied in with acting—a lot of the theater exercises Joan did came out of encounter groups. The director had even brought a woman from Esalen to give a workshop for Joan and the other actors in the play. Joan really liked her. Joan decided to give the Esalen massage and meditation workshop a try.

She wrote for more information about the workshop and sent in her money. But as the day of the workshop grew nearer, she became increasingly ambivalent. Joan really didn't want to go, but felt backed into a corner—she had paid her fee and made a commitment to attend. In a last-ditch effort to get out of going she made a deal with herself: If she awakened on time that morning she'd go to the workshop, and if she didn't, then she wouldn't. To increase the odds in her favor, Joan purposely did not set her alarm clock the night before—she knew it was hard for her to wake up without it. Amazingly, Joan woke up early enough to make it there easily. She took this as a sign that perhaps she was meant to go to this workshop. She felt that each step she took was leading her in a particular, but unfathomable, direction. None of this made any sense to her.

She took the train to the Tarrytown House, where the workshop was being held. As the train pulled into the station, she still had this foreboding feeling that she didn't want to be there. She kept saying to herself, Look, if you hate it, you can just get back on the train and leave; there's no law that says you have to stay. But when she got to the workshop, she was delighted that she had forced herself to go.

As Joan went through the workshop, she discovered the Esalen people had a unique way of working. The focus was on staying in contact with the person you were working on and expanding and exploring your relationship with him. As Joan did the workshop, she thought, This is what I'm good at. I'm very good at connecting with people.

Joan met a woman, whom I'll call Robin, at the workshop and they formed a strong bond. Robin seemed very straightforward and connected to her feelings. Later, Robin invited Joan to be "the body," as they called it, for her lesson. Robin's teacher, whom I will refer to as Bob, taught his students by showing them a movement and then letting them do it to him. Every once in a while, the students would bring in "a body" to work on, so they could show Bob how they performed the different movements. Joan thought it was all very interesting, so interesting, in fact, that she wanted to try doing it herself. At the same time, she kept wondering, Why am I doing this?

Robin worked on Joan for the first fifteen minutes of the half-hour lesson. Then Bob took over because he wanted to make sure that Joan's body was balanced. Joan felt that this work was fabulous, and certainly unlike anything she had previously encountered. Bob asked Joan, "Do you want to learn this? Do you want to take lessons with me?" She answered, "Not really. I don't have a clue as to why I'm drawn to this. To be perfectly honest, I also don't have the time or the money. I'm paying for acting lessons now. I have a job during the day, I do theater at night. I don't even know why I'd want to do it." Private lessons seemed like too much of a commitment to something she didn't even understand.

A couple of months later, Bob sent her a notice that he was giving group classes. She thought, I really like this. I think I'll take a class. It was only ten weeks long, so she could spare the time and money. Joan loved the class. She later realized that she had a lot of awareness and sensitivity even then, when she was still a novice.

Then Joan met Bill, the man with whom she now lives. Joan told him about the massage work she was doing and offered to work on him. At that point she hadn't considered doing massage professionally. Most of her experience came from working on her theater friends when they had headaches. Joan worked on Bill, and he adored it. "Some people take to it and some don't," Joan explained later. "Some people get terribly threatened if I even mention what I do." At that time massage wasn't as prevalent as it is now. Dancers knew about it and some beauty salons provided it, but in general, the whole field of bodywork and awareness is a relatively recent phenomena.

The story of how Joan followed certain leads in her life—based on her dream—is the tale of a woman who allowed herself to be guided by intuition and a belief in a larger intelligence than meets the eye. Even though the dream suggested something that made no sense to her at the time, Joan suspended judgment on whether it might be coming from a higher source. She allied her conscious life with her unconscious, and let her inner guide take the lead. It was no accident that the life events that followed the dream steered Joan in a particular direction. Though skeptical, she took the leads that were presented to her. She let herself be open to what was happening, and trusted that she might be moving on the right path. Her skepticism was partly due to her preconceptions about massage. She later discovered that this field promised an entirely new experience and understanding than she had been aware of at the time of the dream.

Another striking thing about this dream is that the message was so strongly and clearly stated, in black and white. When a message like that appears in a dream, take heed, even if it makes no sense to you at the time. The message is similar to what is commonly called "the writing on the wall." But in this case the writing was on the blackboard. Most of us associate blackboards with school. Note also that Joan's message referred to "learning." That meant it could be connected to an early period of her life, as if the seeds were planted back in childhood. It's also significant that the message said "I want." Those are strong, assertive words, indicating a specific desire. When a message like that comes to us in a dream, it is expressing something very deep within us. Joan's wish was eventually fulfilled, but it didn't happen with just a click of the fingers. That kind of magic only appears in children's fairy tales. Joan's wish came true because she took the many necessary steps to actualize it in the material world. Jung said that it was when dreamers expressed the images and symbols of their dreams in their waking lives that the dream had the power to change the dreamer.

Another reason Joan paid special attention to this dream is that she understands things by first visualizing them. As a child she learned through seeing things written on blackboards. Her dream used a familiar setting associated with learning to point out that she should learn massage.

Joan recalled working on Bill one night. She was wearing a blue-and-white Indian dress at the time, and it reminded her of a Japanese fabric she had seen. She looked down and saw her hands—they appeared very small. She thought, No wonder this is so familiar; I have done this before. Joan realized that she had done this work in a past life in Japan, which explained her quick and powerful connection to it.

About two years later, Joan took a second series of classes. By that time she had come to hate her job as a caseworker for the city. She felt she wasn't right for it because she got too emotionally involved. Every day she went home upset. Joan also wasn't making any money through acting. She knew that there had to be something in this big world that she would love doing. She didn't want to just look for another job, because at least with this one she was able to schedule the time for acting classes.

What Joan really wanted was work that she loved that also paid a decent salary. She loved acting—but couldn't earn a living doing it. She prayed, asking God to bring something forward for her. And God did. While working on Bill, she thought about Bob, her teacher who had a private massage practice. Other people did that work for a living; maybe she could do it, too. Joan explored her options. She called the Swedish Institute. She considered becoming a Rolfer and called the Rolfing Institute. She also thought about becoming a physical therapist, but then decided she did not have the emotional wherewithal that profession required.

Then she contacted Bob. His immediate response was, "When do you want to come up?" Joan answered, "Next week," and set up an appointment. When Joan arrived for their meeting, Bob got right down to business. "I want to see what you remember," he announced. "Before we go any further, I need to know if you have the talent for it, if you're the right person to do it." He hopped up on the table and Joan worked on him. When she finished, he said, "I think you could be really good at this. As a matter of fact, I think you could be great."

Joan began studying with Bob. Her training period was longer than any other student he'd had because of her voracious appetite for knowledge. As soon as she learned something, she invariably asked, "What else do you have to teach me?"

Eventually Joan started taking on clients, as a sideline to her main job. A year later she had more clients than she could handle. At a friend's instigation, Joan quit her job and devoted herself full-time to her practice. Twenty-three years later, she's completely devoted to her work.

All sorts of things have come to Joan through this work, including lots of publicity. As she became increasingly involved with her work, it seemed that all the other aspects of her life clicked into place and were perfectly aligned. Joan felt that she had come home, that she was doing exactly what she was meant to do.

Although people commented on her success, Joan never thought about it in those terms. This was simply what she loved to do. Since Bob had a lot of clients, it seemed natural and unremarkable that she would, too. Bob later told her that he had never seen anyone build up a practice as quickly as she did. Her clients literally multiplied. She would see two people one week, and the following week they'd each say, "Oh, I have two friends who want to see you." Those people then referred more people, and her practice quickly expanded. It wasn't long before Joan discovered that even if she worked twenty-four hours a day, seven days a week, she still couldn't see everybody who wanted to come to her. She also realized that if she was going to keep doing this, she had to take some time off for herself. She was forced to sit down and figure out exactly how many people she could handle and then stick to that schedule. Joan felt that her work was God's gift to her, and considered herself enormously blessed for discovering her purpose in life.

Since Joan was convinced that people do many different things while in the dream state, such as traveling and studying, it was no wonder she took her "learning" dream seriously. The dream about massage, Joan believed, was also connected to a high school memory. She was a senior at the time, and other students were discussing their postgraduation plans—what they were going to do, whether they were going to college, what their college major would be, and so on. Joan said that the only things she wanted to do was to sit in cafés and talk to people and give them love. She really thought that was the job for her. One nun replied, "But there's no job like that," to which Joan responded, "Then there should be." Joan told me that she would like to write this nun now and say, "Dear Sister Grace Anthony, I found that job. I call it deep-muscle therapy." Through her work, Joan has fulfilled her high school goal of expressing love as a career.

"That dream continues to have a significant impact on my life," Joan said recently. "Every once in a while, when I get anxious and wonder, Should I be doing something else? somebody comes into my practice and asks, 'How did you get into this work?' I tell them the story and it so calms me, because it reminds me that spirit is guiding me, that there is a plan. It's been said, 'Many are called, few are chosen, and fewer still choose back.' I'm not passive about this. It's a question of choosing back, and not just once, but again and again. What I love about this dream is it continues to enhance my life. It reminds me that if I do what's in front of me one hundred percent, my destiny will bring the next step forward."

Symbol for Your Dream Dictionary:

Message on blackboard: A clear, succinct, and unalterable message. It's black and white, with no in-between. Pay attention to any message presented to you this way in your dream.

Exercise: Dream Incubation

Do this exercise before you go to sleep.

Sit quietly and think about a situation that currently

concerns you. Place a book and a pen next to your bed, then lie down and create a question that specifically addresses what you need to know. Repeat the question over and over in your mind as you go to sleep. This popular dream exercise is commonly called the Incubation Method, but there's one additional, important step that was contributed by Joan Witkowski. Add a glass of water to the objects on your night table. Tell yourself that when you awaken, you will take a sip of water and then write down whatever details or impressions you remember from your dream.

Why is the sip of water important? "The sip of water is to key in the memories," Joan explained. "When someone believes, 'I can never remember dreams. I can't do this. I won't do it because I'm afraid,' the glass of water is an anchor. It's part of the programming. It's a connection, like people writing themselves a note or a key word to remember something. The water can trigger the memory.

"When you awaken, take a sip of water and write. You may remember a dream, or you may not. Write something either way. Even if you wake up groggy and a little cranky, you could still remember something—a street, for instance, or a person, from your dream. That's a beginning. When you start writing, other images will appear. Don't be disappointed if your message isn't as clear-cut and obvious as 'I want to learn massage' written on a blackboard. Answers frequently come in stages or phases."

In conclusion, Joan's experience is an example of what can happen when people listen to their dreams. Dreams are a source of great wisdom, and the people who allow themselves to be guided by their dreams may find it easier to fulfill their purpose in life. Through our dreams, our lives take on a new meaning. To quote

Jung: "Whoever nurtures this contact between conscious and unconscious will, in time, experience a great spiritual and moral release of tension, his inner oppositions will be lessened; he will take root in his instinct and gain that sense of security and support which is beyond the reach of the intellect and will with its oscillating relations. At the same time there will develop in him an undreamed-of fullness of life that expands rather than shrinks with age because the instincts and values are being truly lived."

Thus dreams can offer us guidance throughout our lifetime.

FOUR

The Rapist at the Top of the Steps

The dreamer, Patricia, was a middle-aged woman who had been frigid her entire adult life. The following dream changed all of that.

DREAM: *I leave my house. A man comes up my steps and grabs me so that I cannot move. He puts his hands on my breasts. He's very big and although I scream and struggle, I can't fight him off. Two other men are standing on the street below and remain indifferent to my cries. The man puts his fingers on my nipples, which become hard. I somehow make the sensation disappear, and my nipples become soft again. I am terrified and enraged, too.*

In the next scene I am in a therapy group, telling everyone my dream. My brother is lying on a bed opposite me; this is not where he is supposed to be. He's supposed to be on a bed over to the right. I freeze up inside but try not to show my reaction, still acting calm and unruffled. But, feeling the group's support, I conjure up the courage to tell him he's not supposed to be where he is. He moves over. And the group leader takes his place on the bed. The group leader tells me I am dramatizing the story in order to

*get the group's attention. I protest, shocked that the
therapist has turned against me. And then I realize
the person I depend upon to support me has betrayed
me. Someone from the group who has not been listening carefully asks, "Did he [the man] touch you?" I
do not answer the question because I feel ashamed. I
wake up.*

Patricia knew immediately that there was a connection between this dream and her unconscious pattern of
turning off her physical sensations during sex. In waking life, Patricia was unable to sustain a relationship
with a man because of her frigidity. She always thought
it was because her older brother had once tried to molest her when she was six. Under the guise of showing
her a newborn calf, the fifteen-year-old had lured her
into a barn on their grandparents' farm. He tried unsuccessfully to put his penis inside her, and threatened to
feed her to the horses if she told anyone. She was terrified, but fortunately her grandfather came into the
barn at that moment. From then on, she tried never to
be alone with her brother. And she never told anybody.

She was puzzled by the part in the dream where she
made the sensation in her nipples disappear, but then remembered an experience with a child molester when she
was ten years old. There was something in that childhood experience that was identical to the dream. The
molester had touched her and she had stiffened, so that
she was not aware of any physical sensation—which
suggests that she might have had physical sensations that
she tried to ward off. She also thought that if she didn't
react to the molester he wouldn't be encouraged to continue what he was doing.

I asked her to take some deep breaths and imagine
herself back in that same place where she met the child

molester. To help make the experience more immediate, I asked her what she was wearing and to describe her surroundings. She recalled that she was wearing a blue-and-white checked pinafore dress. She was in the middle of a path surrounded by large trees and thick foliage. She was hurrying because she had left school late and was expected at home. All the other children had gone home earlier. As she crossed the empty playground behind the school and scurried down the steps leading to a dead-end street, she spotted an old Chevrolet parked at the dead-end street. Nobody was sitting inside the car. A month before, when she had also left school late, she had met the owner of that car. Again she was alone, because all the other children had gone home earlier. The owner of the car was standing by a tree and began to ask her about the nuts on the ground beneath the tree. She didn't see any nuts, and she didn't know why he was there; he didn't seem to be a parent waiting to pick up his child. And he appeared very strange to the little girl. There was something about the way he spoke to her that was insincere, unreal. His questions didn't seem normal to her. In fact, she wondered if he asked her about the nuts because he himself was nuts.

So, spotting the car, she hurried down the steps and through the shortcut that the children frequently used, thinking that she could avoid the man. After taking a few steps onto the path, she saw him. She thought of turning around and running, but she realized he could easily grab her, especially if he knew she was afraid of him. Even at ten, she knew she must act as if everything were normal, and she made an effort to hide her fear.

He told her he had just seen a rabbit and was looking for it. He kneeled down and began feeling the ground, pretending that he could trace the rabbit tracks that way.

Then he picked up an old rusty saw that Patricia had seen on the path before. She wondered if he was going to kill her. But he put down the saw, saying, "This won't help." Patricia was relieved but also thought he was giving her a warning not to disobey him. "Come over here," he ordered her. "Let's find the rabbit together." She obediently went over to him. He motioned her to stand closer. Then he put his hand under her dress and began running his hand over her body. Patricia remembered contracting her buttocks when he touched her, either to ward off his touch or to stop sensation, just as she had in the dream where the man touched her nipples. He put his other hand in his pants. She wasn't sure what he was doing, but a few seconds later he let her go. Not until we discussed the dream did Patricia suspect that he had had an orgasm.

It had begun to rain lightly. "It's raining," Patricia said guardedly, wondering what was going to happen next. "Yes," he replied. "You can go," he told her. "Don't get wet." She was surprised that he let her go, and walked away at a normal pace until she got out of his sight. Then she ran as fast as she could all the way home.

When Patricia got home, she told the nanny what had happened. Her parents were not at home. When her mother came home, Patricia didn't say anything about the man. She already had the feeling that she had done something wrong or that the man could still follow her and kill her. But the nanny said to her in front of Patricia's mother, "Tell your mother about that funny man." "What funny man?" her mother asked suspiciously. Patricia reluctantly told her mother the story. Patricia overheard her mother talking quietly to her father when he came home from work. An hour later detectives came to the house and questioned Patricia about the man. They advised her mother to pick her up every day after school.

On one such occasion, many months later, the old Chevy showed up at the dead-end street again. But Patricia's mother had gotten there in time to take down the man's license plate number. With this information, the police were able to identify the man, who had an extensive record of molesting children.

After the incident, Patricia recalled, she'd had recurring nightmares of the front door of the house opening; she would try to lock the door but a man on the other side would force the door open. Patricia would awaken in terror. The nightmares reflected the fear that Patricia had buried; she felt helpless to prevent a man from violating her. (The house in her dream symbolized her self.) The only way she could prevent further violation was to shut off her own physical sensations. However, this did not really work, as indicated by her nightmares. She also had recurring dreams of being chased by an evil man.

As she was reliving the incident with the molester, I asked Patricia if she could remember feeling afraid. She said she couldn't. She only acted in self-protection; she wasn't aware of feeling fear. I asked her to imagine the same scene happening to someone else, to be an onlooker observing this man trapping and molesting a ten-year-old girl. At that Patricia became very frightened. I had tried this technique, realizing that the incident was probably too threatening for her to experience it firsthand. Only by artificially creating a safer space, with herself as an onlooker rather than a participant, did she begin to feel the fear she had repressed, the fear she needed to feel in order to undo her frigidity.

After retrieving this memory of child molestation, she began to observe how she stopped sensations whenever she was touched sexually, even though the sensation was something she consciously desired now. As a child there was no one to protect her from this unwanted invasion of her body, her very being; the only way to keep someone out was to control her own physical reactions.

In the dream, Patricia was not only terrified of the man who touched her nipples but also enraged. She was too frightened to allow herself to express her anger. But when she remembered the barn incident with her brother, she was able for the first time to feel anger.

The dream offered Patricia, as dreams often do, a solution to her dilemma. In the dream she conjured up the courage to tell her brother he's out of order (in the wrong place), believing she would be supported by the group. In order for Patricia to undo the damage of her childhood molestations, she must be able to verbalize them, protest them, feel the fear and the rage. Repression of these feelings led to repression of other feelings, including sexual ones. Freeing her fear and rage would also release the sexual feelings. She was vowed to silence by her brother, but her courage to finally speak up in the dream showed her willingness to confront him at last.

This impulse to speak up was a very positive sign. However, she was betrayed by the group leader who took her brother's place on the bed. The location of the group leader is not to be overlooked. I asked Patricia if this group leader reminded her of anyone, and she initially said no. However, in describing his physical characteristics, she remembered a boss who had made a pass at her, which caused her to leave her job. At that time the concept of sexual harrassment did not exist, and women were helpless against it. The appearance of the untrustworthy group leader in Patricia's dream is evidence of her wavering trust. He actually replaced the brother who had molested her, by taking his place in the dream. She could not yet depend on men.

The last part of the dream—where the group member asked Patricia, "Did he touch you?"—brought out Patricia's shame and guilt at having been touched by the molester. Such is the damage inflicted by child molesters. The dream revealed to Patricia that *she* felt shame and blamed *herself* when she was sexually abused. Once Patricia had this information, she began to understand that her shame was unfounded, and that she did not have to conceal her erotic feelings behind shame. As her frigidity began to melt, Patricia began accepting her sexual impulses. She no longer fears that she is doomed to a life without intimacy. She resumed her relationship with the man she had recently left and is able, for the first time, to be truly close with him.

Symbols for Your Dream Dictionary:

House: Self.

Steps: Passageway between levels of awareness. Steps descending are getting closer to the unconscious.

Group: Reflecting an unacceptable point of view of the dreamer. Public opinion.

Bed: Where sex is performed.

Right: Morality.

Leader: Authority, parent.

Non-listener: Indifference.

Dream Exercise: Tell the Dream from Another Character's Point of View

A well-proven dream theory is that every character in the dream is some representation of ourselves. It is usually a part of ourselves that we project onto others or dissociate from ourselves. The purpose of telling your dream from another character's point of view is to externalize an aspect of self you don't care to identify with, or to express feelings that make you too vulnerable if you claim them as your own. Experiencing your buried feelings through another dream character is a way not only to understand your dream but also to see aspects of yourself you may have denied. By accepting these aspects as your own, you become a more integrated human being.

Few of us are fully in touch with all our feelings, especially all the time; they tend to come out when we least expect them. We may catch ourselves, for example, having intense empathy for a character in a play or movie. Or we may hate some other character without knowing why. Patients have told me from time to time they've burst into tears viewing a particular television drama and were concerned that they were overreacting. But they weren't overreacting; they were giving expression to their own unconscious pain, now reflected externally. The work of art was able to release repressed wishes or feelings in the onlooker. And this was fruitful material for the therapy.

Just as we can discover our denied feelings in a character in a movie, play, or book, we can make similar discoveries in a dream. Therefore, telling the dream through the voice of another character can give expression to an unconscious aspect of yourself.

By doing this exercise you will get a glimpse of yourself as others may see you, for you will stop disowning the parts of yourself that exist in your unconscious.

FIVE

The Attacker

This patient, whom I'll call Beth, had always felt that there was something about her that turned other people off. What was so frustrating to her was that she had no idea what it was. Relentless self-examination provided no clues. She knew she was smart, articulate, and witty, and yet it was obvious that something was seriously wrong, for she had felt excluded, ignored, and rejected by other people for as long as she could remember. She claimed that people treated her as if she was invisible, invading her personal space until she was forced to step back and relinquish her spot. They turned their backs on her at parties, forming tight circles that had no room for her but magically opened up whenever anyone else approached. It seemed as if she was always peering over someone's shoulder in an attempt to be a part of the conversation, but no one ever acknowledged her presence with even so much as a glance. On those rare occasions when people did recognize her existence and appeared to listen to her, someone invariably interrupted her in the middle of a sentence and abruptly changed the subject. Without fail, others in the group responded by instantly and eagerly diverting their attention to this other person. When Beth approached someone standing by themselves at a party or a club, she was greeted with, as she put it, "the same warmth and encouragement that a cockroach on the dinner table would receive." Beth was so humiliated by these incidents that she finally stopped attending social gatherings.

I asked her to describe the source of her problem. "There's something primal and fundamental in me that's bad," she explained. "I'm like an animal that has the wrong scent. Other people smell that I'm different and automatically shy away from me without consciously knowing why." Years of therapy had produced no explanations or solutions to her problem. By the time she came to me at age forty, she was resigned to her painful fate and just wanted help in coping with it. Everything changed, however, after she had the following dream:

DREAM: *A woman with long fingernails attacks me. She is weaker than me and I think I can fend her off. But she claws at me with such unrelenting energy that I eventually become exhausted. I use up my last iota of strength and finally give up—I just can't raise my arms one more time. She viciously swarms all over me, raking me with her sharp nails until I'm covered in blood. There are other people around, but no one hears my screams or tries to help. I realize that she's never going to stop—she's going to shred me until I disappear. I wake up in terror.*

I asked Beth to lie on her back and reenter the dream. She got comfortable, took a few deep breaths, and immediately turned her attention to a key detail in the dream—the long fingernails. Obviously ashamed, she confessed that she had bitten her fingernails as a child. Her mother tried to break her of the habit by frequently comparing her stubby, ugly nails with her twin sister's perfectly manicured nails. Beth eventually stopped biting her nails, but remained self-conscious about her hands.

Beth went on to say that she and her identical twin sister, Polly, did not enjoy a close relationship. Indeed, they fought so much that by fifth grade they had to be put in separate schools. Aside from their looks they had little in common. Beth was a shy, sensitive, and bookish girl who was regarded as "weird" and "queer" by her classmates. Her interests, priorities, and ideas were so different from her peers' that she felt as if she was from a different planet. After several degrading and unsuccessful attempts to fit in, Beth gave up and went to the other extreme. She exaggerated and flaunted her differences, making sure the way she looked, acted, and talked was the exact opposite of everyone else. That gave her the illusion of being in control of the situation, an aggressor who intentionally caused the estrangement, rather than the helpless victim of everyone else's rejection.

Polly, on the other hand, was as "normal" as could be. She effortlessly fit in with even the snobbiest kids and seemed to instinctively know all the right things to say and do. She didn't hide her disdain for Beth—and was so embarrassed by her that she refused to be seen in public with her.

The long fingernails indicated to Beth that the woman in her dream was her twin sister. This realization brought back memories of their relationship as children. She listed examples of her sister's abuse—Polly blackmailed her, strangled her, punched her, and humiliated her in public—in the dispassionate tone of someone reading a shopping list. When I commented on her lack of emotion she seemed surprised. It was my impression that she was repressing her hurt over her sister's rejection, but Beth adamantly denied it, assuring me that they had "hated each other equally" and that she had never wanted or needed her sister's acceptance.

The session ended before we could complete our work on the dream, so we continued working on it at our next session. During that session, Beth discovered that the more she allowed herself to feel the dream, the more connections she found to her sister. She told me that her sister had tried to kill her from the moment they were born. Polly, who was born first, was a breech baby. Her umbilical cord was wrapped around Beth's neck and nearly strangled her. Beth was convinced that this was somehow intentional, and cited her sister's subsequent practice of choking her until she passed out as proof. She also mentioned that Polly had gone home from the hospital right away, while she had to remain in an incubator for ten days. According to their mother, Polly had been a completely content baby until Beth was brought home from the hospital. Polly started screaming the moment Beth was placed in the crib next to hers—and didn't stop until Beth began to cry. For the first few months of her life, Beth cried incessantly. No matter how much she was held or what anyone did, she was inconsolable. Beth's mother later admitted that Beth's nonstop wailing literally drove her out of the house.

As Beth expressed how much her sister hated her, she also explained the reason for it: Polly hated being a twin. Even as an adult, Polly didn't forgive their mother for dressing them alike as small children. When they were in their thirties, the two sisters reunited for a brief visit after many years of separation. While at a supermarket, a clerk asked them if they were twins. Speaking in unison, Beth answered "yes" and Polly said "no."

In order for Beth to derive the full benefit of her dream, I asked her to reexperience the feelings in her dream. How did it feel, I asked her, when her sister attacked her? She said that she felt overwhelmed by the assault, frustrated that no one came to her rescue, and ultimately resigned to being destroyed. Conspicuously absent from the list were fear and hurt. When the session ended I asked Beth to do a writing exercise during the week, which consisted of "talking" to her sister about the dream by asking her questions, and then answering them as if she were her sister. When she came to the next session, she brought her written dialogue with her. This is what she wrote:

"Why are you attacking me?"

"I must destroy you in order to survive."

"Why must you destroy me to survive?"

"Because you have things that are missing in me. The only way I might get them and become whole is for you to die."

"I don't understand. We're twins, we're supposed to have a special connection. Look at the twins on 'The Patty Duke Show' and in the Hayley Mills movie. That's how we should be. Maybe you don't feel whole because you refuse to be close to me."

"I will never be close to you. I will do everything I can to be as different and distant from you as possible. I refuse to be a twin. I hate you more than anything else in the world and I wish you would die."

"Isn't there anything I can do to change your feelings? I want my twin sister."

"No. It doesn't matter who you are or what you do. To me, you'll always be a constant reminder of everything I'm missing. You're not a person, you're some awful thing that should be destroyed. Looking at you makes me hate myself. The fact that you're my twin sister, that you're alive, is all the reason I need to despise you."

"What exactly is it that you're missing and I have?"

"You have everything it takes to be a complete person. I can't even describe what that is, because I don't have it. I just feel the emptiness, these big holes inside me where that stuff should be. It's like you got two of some things and I didn't get any. You got my stuff."

"How can you be missing so much when it's so easy for you to be popular and fit in? I'm the freak. If anyone is missing something, it's me."

"It's all an act. I learned to compensate for what I didn't have a long time ago, and thank God I got good at it. I don't have the luxury of doing whatever I want, like you. I have to conform, follow the party line, so that no one discovers how much I'm missing. I don't have the stuff that would make me be a unique individual. You have my share of that as well as your own, which is why you're so weird. You have too much and I don't have enough."

"I didn't intentionally take that from you."

"What difference does that make? The bottom line is that you have it and I don't. It might be better if I thought you took it on purpose, because that might mean I had the power to get it back. But there's nothing I can do about this situation."

"If you can't get that stuff back, then why do you want to kill me?"

"Because maybe if you died that stuff would be transferred to me. At the very least, I wouldn't have to see you walking around with what belongs to me. I wouldn't be continually reminded that I was cheated out of being a whole person."

"When did you start feeling that you were missing something?"

"The moment you came home from the hospital. Up until then I thought I was fine, but seeing you showed me all the things I was missing. You ruined my life. I'll never be happy because of you."

"I hate feeling so powerless, like there's nothing I can do to make you accept me."

"You're right, there is nothing you can do to make me accept you. I never will. I'm glad you feel powerless; now you have a taste of what I go through every day. I hope it hurts you a lot. My only regret is that no matter how much I hurt you, it will never compare to the pain I feel because of you."

Beth was in tears by the time she finished reading the dialogue out loud. She was rejected from day one by the person who should have been closest to her, who should have loved and understood her the most. She felt she was set up to expect a certain closeness—"After all, we were together literally since the day we were conceived"—and then arbitrarily denied it. There was no way she could change things or rectify the situation. She was helpless. Her sister completely negated her as a person. That kind of insurmountable rejection seemed almost unnatural to Beth. Polly cheated her out of the experience of being a twin or even having a sister. Beth hated that she had so much power over her: "I was so vulnerable and she was so cruel. I can't imagine a worse way to start your life. I feel like she irreparably damaged me."

Beth blamed herself for Polly's hatred. She internalized it. Since she never understood why Polly rejected her and why she couldn't make Polly like her, she felt that there must be something intrinsically wrong with her. Since she could never figure out what that was, she felt insecure and defenseless. "All my life," Beth said, "I've been like someone who unknowingly tucked the back of her skirt into her panty hose and doesn't understand why everyone is laughing at her. No one will let me in on the joke."

Beth projected her feelings of being innately defective onto others. All her life she used that belief to rationalize and explain why she couldn't connect with other people. Now she sees that each time she did that she strengthened that belief. Unconsciously she sent out messages to everyone that something was wrong with her, and she believed they acted accordingly, that it was a self-fulfilling prophecy.

"The woman in my dream was not just my sister, but also my own belief that something was wrong with me. I think the dream was a warning that my self, my very being, was being destroyed by that perception. I had given it too much power.

"It's very clear to me now that there is nothing wrong with me. The reason I could never explain this fundamental flaw was because it never existed. My sister rejected me because of her problems; it had nothing to do with me or who I am. She would have rejected anyone who was her twin. The only reason people might think there is something wrong with me is because I send out the message that there is. I think I made a habit of unconsciously apologizing for myself, so people just assumed that I must have done something wrong.

"I feel like an enormous weight has been lifted off my shoulders. The mystery that has consumed my life has been solved. All the pieces have fallen into place and everything finally makes sense. It's so simple and clear. I feel a calmness and confidence I never had before. It's unbelievable what a difference this has made. I can't understand why it took me so long to figure this out; it seems so obvious now. I guess it's a real lesson about the way unconscious or unquestioned assumptions can blind you to the truth."

Beth later came up with another interpretation for the dream: The attacker perhaps represented her true self, which was trying to destroy the insidious part of her that said she was fundamentally flawed. "In that case," Beth said, "the dream isn't a nightmare but rather a good omen."

A few weeks after that session, Beth informed me that she had had a very interesting talk with her mother about her sister. She prefaced her remarks by saying that Polly had never shared her feelings about being a twin with her and that she hadn't known whether the feelings that her sister "expressed" in her written exercise truly represented her sister's emotions. During her conversation with her mother, however, Beth learned that her sister had indeed always envied Beth's creativity and had felt that parts of her were missing. Her mother had explained that as a child Polly had worked very hard to be accepted by her peers, strictly conforming to the social norms in a desperate effort to be included in the "best" clique. Beth felt this information validated her insights and confirmed her belief that she had solved the mystery that had plagued her for so long.

Symbols for Your Dream Dictionary:
Fingernails: Weapons.
Blood: Life force.

Exercise: Have a Conversation with an Important Dream Character

Characters in our dreams are often disguised facets of

ourselves that are too painful or threatening to acknowledge. Writing a dialogue with a dream character is an excellent way to circumvent our barriers and give that part of ourselves a "voice" to explain its message and purpose. These insights can bring us right into the feelings we may have been avoiding. Ask the dream character specific questions like "Why are you in my dream?" and "Why did you behave the way you did?"

When answering these questions, step into that character's shoes, so to speak, and write whatever pops into your mind. Don't censor or judge yourself or try to construct "logical" answers. Your immediate response is the most accurate one. If no response comes to mind, write "I don't know," and then ask the character more questions, such as "Why don't you know?" and "What do you think it means?" Continue the conversation until all your questions have been answered and there's nothing more to talk about. If more questions arise later, go back and ask them. You'll be surprised by all the buried feelings, information, and insights that will surface through your conversations. The result may be a transformative experience, like Beth's.

SIX

My Volvo Disappears

DREAM: *I park my Volvo on the street in an unfamiliar neighborhood. When I look for it later, I can't find it. I walk up and down the streets full of anxiety. My car has disappeared. Desperately I yell out, "Where is my car?"*

The dreamer, whom I shall call Alan, had this dream about one year into therapy. He described himself as a person who never dreams, which made this dream even more significant. Alan learned at a young age to suppress his feelings because his early experiences were too painful to deal with.

Alan talked about himself with an air of detachment; he appeared to think and act according to someone else's dictates. Alan was a lawyer who went to his office every day like clockwork. If he couldn't do exactly what his clients wanted, he felt a terrible sense of failure. He was anxious all the time from trying to please them and worrying they wouldn't like what he'd done. It stopped him from enjoying his work, something he'd spent years trying to perfect. He questioned why he needed to work if it made him so anxious. His work now offered him no satisfaction, just turmoil.

He wondered who this disapproving god he was trying to please was, and why had he given himself away to Him, or to It? It felt more like *It*, Alan explained, because no one, including himself, seemed to be benefiting from his struggle.

Alan resignedly told me that he didn't know why he did what he did. For example, he didn't know why he married his wife. He didn't love her. He admitted he was attracted to her once, but no more. "So why did you marry her?" I asked. "To please her," he replied. "To please my family—my dad, who had died years before my marriage. She makes me look good, but I don't think that's enough. She's never around, which, in a sense, is a relief. She's always off acting in some regional theater. When she is around, I can't tell if she's acting or being herself. Who is she anyway?"

Alan had such a wish to please that it overrode everything in his life. At the same time, he was also very dependent. When he asked himself out loud if he would be better off without his wife, he immediately became frightened. Having her gave him at least a sense of security—someone was there. Alan admitted he was terrified of being alone—out there in orbit, with no one knowing or caring whether he lived or died. That feeling was worse than feeling cut off when he was with her and uncomfortable when she asked him to say, "I love you," even though he didn't mean it. His wife was the one thread that connected him to the world. It made him nervous that the thread that connected him to her was so fragile it could easily break.

The fact that there seemed to be no way out of these painful feelings filled him with despair. He wondered if this was the best he could do. I thought to myself that the only way out for Alan was *in*—to his feelings. Alan was an expert at keeping his feelings at bay. One of his defenses was to keep himself so busy that he could forget about his loneliness. This need to keep busy began much earlier in his life. In high school Alan joined the Drama Club, the Science Club, and the Nature Club. His fellow students thought he was a nerd, one of those guys who made A's but had no social graces. He never dated. While he knew people made fun of him, he did everything he could to shut that knowledge out, including keeping himself so busy that he wouldn't have time to think about it.

His father kept busy all the time, too, so Alan reasoned if he followed in his father's footsteps, his father was bound to like him. He hoped that his father would at least approve of all his activity. When Alan's father wasn't teaching, he worked in his tool shop. As a boy, Alan visited him there. Alan loved being in the tool shop with his father, but he was also uneasy because he wasn't sure his father wanted him there. Alan hoped his father would show him how to make a table or something. *Anything*. But his sudden appearance in the tool shop only jarred his father. Alan's presence seemed to distract his father—he invariably just mumbled a few words and then ignored his son. He made it clear he didn't enjoy Alan's company, and finally Alan would leave.

After a while, that didn't hurt Alan anymore. He reasoned that his father just needed to be alone to concentrate. But Alan still wondered why his father told him to help his mother set the table whenever Alan asked him to take a walk with him. When Alan's younger brother wanted to walk with his father, their father happily stopped what he was doing to accompany him. Why, Alan wondered, did his father's customary angry expression turn into a smile whenever Alan's brother entered the room? "Why did he like my brother but not me?" Alan asked. It was apparent that Alan needed to rationalize his feelings away because he felt so rejected.

Alan's father taught Alan to work hard. "No time for play," his father said. "That doesn't build character." According to his father, every moment had to be spent in some productive pursuit.

If only his father could see him now, Alan thought. If only he could see how hard he worked. Yet Alan wasn't sure where his life was going. He didn't know if law was the vocation he wanted to pursue forever. He didn't really know what motivated him—was it money or recognition? If it was the latter, then recognition by whom? After all, he lamented, he didn't have any friends.

Alan had graduated from law school with honors. His father wasn't at his graduation—he'd died shortly before. His father didn't attend his high school graduation, either. Alan never forgave his father for that. Alan even felt that his father bailed out on him by dying before he graduated law school; why couldn't he have waited for him to graduate? Alan had desperately wanted to make his father proud. His law school graduation was his only chance, and his father blew it. Or did he, Alan, blow it? It seemed to Alan as if all his work, all his efforts to please his father, had withered away like a starfish washed up on the sand. Alan said he felt catatonic when he graduated. He numbly accepted the congratulations of his family and instructors, but since his father was missing, Alan felt like it was all a waste. He had worked so hard for nothing.

Whenever we met, Alan appeared eager and cheerful, but I could sense his underlying malaise. During our first session, he claimed that he was fairly happy, and that he was eager to try therapy because it could be an interesting experience. (Who would come to therapy out of mere curiosity?) Alan was a strange combination of detachment and eagerness to please. He had very little insight into himself and coped with life by denying his feelings.

I wondered what his basis was for describing himself as happy. He had no friends, no social life, no hobbies or outside interests. He was miserable with his wife and escaped life by being a workaholic who stayed in his office even when there was no work to be done. His assertion of happiness was proof of how out of touch he was with his feelings. It wasn't long before he admitted he worked long hours just to avoid feeling he had nothing in his life—no real relationship, no future, nothing to look forward to.

To justify his unrewarding marriage, Alan admitted that he stayed in situations long after he should have left. In fact, he waited for the situation to get rid of him. For example, he only moved to a better apartment because his lease ran out and the landlord forced him to move. Otherwise he'd still be there.

When I asked him if he ever told his wife how he felt, he confessed he was unable to confront anyone or anything that distressed him. He once waited a whole year before billing a client, and even then did so only with great trepidation, fearing that he would upset the client.

Later, he described in more detail the fear he felt when he was alone. He felt such emptiness, hopelessness, and separation that even talking about it during the session agitated him. It was like being in a cell, he said, in isolation. The world disappeared and no one knew he was alive. However, being in the world was often worse than being in a cell, because then he had to endure the pain of seeing couples who obviously cared deeply for each other. That underscored the emptiness in his own life.

If he left his wife, he was convinced that he wouldn't

be able to meet people or talk to them. He was sure he would bore others. In fact, he thought his problems were so small that he couldn't even interest a therapist. Alan was always afraid he'd run out of things to say during our sessions.

Alan's apathy and ennui ran so deep that he couldn't enjoy his triumphs. He had just been accepted as a partner in a prestigious law firm. While he had prayed that would happen, he didn't feel excited when his wish was fulfilled. No *thing* and no *one* excited him. That was the condition of his life when his turning-point dream occurred.

When Alan told me his dream, I put myself in his place and imagined how I would feel if I had had that dream. The dream made me feel frantic because I had lost something valuable. So I asked Alan to tell me about the lost object—the Volvo.

The Volvo, he said, was a car his father had given him when he was in high school. He loved this car and took excellent care of it. When he went away to college he lent it to his younger brother. He later found out that his brother sold the car. Alan cried at the news. "That was the only time in my life I cried," he said, "except for when my father died. I couldn't believe how much pain my father's death caused me. We were never close. He never seemed particularly interested in me. I never felt anything I ever did pleased him. But his death was the most painful experience of my life."

Alan's associations to the Volvo revealed the meaning of the dream. When his father gave him the Volvo, Alan was ecstatic. Maybe it meant that his father cared for him after all. The car was the only evidence that even suggested that his father might love him, which is why its loss was such a terrible blow. With this connection I began to understand things that were previously unclear to me, such as his frequent complaints about therapy. Alan complained that I didn't give him enough interpretation and feedback. He thought I was bored. He felt it was my job to make him feel more enthusiastic about life. Perhaps I was the wrong therapist for him, he said. Why didn't I challenge him more?

I realized these complaints were not really about me—they reflected his father's lack of interest in him. I saw that his father's lack of interest made him feel hopeless about his own life. How could anyone, even his therapist, be interested in him? How could anyone be impressed with him, his work, or anything he did? Everything looked bleak. How could he feel motivated when his father never thought he was anyone special? His pleasant veneer hid the orphan inside, the child no one ever paid attention to.

Alan had recently told me he felt he was going to fail in his work by doing something really wrong. He had felt tense all week and wanted these feelings to disappear. When I asked him what he needed to make these feelings go away, he answered, "Outside acknowledgment." That response clearly indicated that the Volvo in Alan's dream represented his father's love. Alan unconsciously believed that he could never love himself until he found his father's love.

When I told this to Alan, he replied that it made sense to him intellectually but he couldn't feel it emotionally. How could I help Alan get in touch with his feelings? I had to find a way to help Alan open up to his emotions. Until a person actually experiences the feelings in the dream, the dream's impact is minimal. In our next session, he admitted that he might be emotionally blocked from feeling the pain about his father, and that the sudden death of his father—a man who was emotionally unavailable even when alive—made it impossible for him to ever win his love.

Alan's father died just when Alan thought he had another chance to connect with his father on a new level. Although his father never showed any interest in anything Alan had done in the past, he was curious about the law—which was what Alan was studying. When his father died, Alan wept as he had never wept before. He didn't know why it affected him so deeply, but he must have unconsciously known that when his father died it was also the death of any hope or chance that he and his father would ever bond. This was one of the biggest tragedies in Alan's life. However, he was so disconnected from his feelings that his own tears surprised him. He had no idea his father meant so much to him.

But Alan acknowledged that he had blocked his feelings, and so I took the process a step further. I asked him to pretend his father was in the room and tell him how angry he was that he never made him feel special. Alan conjured up an image of his father in his mind, but he said he couldn't tell him he was angry. Instead he defended him. "He did his best," Alan argued. I told Alan he was protecting his father and not feeling his own needs. Suddenly Alan began to cry. "I just wanted more," he said, sobbing. A typical childhood scene popped into his mind—having dinner with his family. Alan experienced himself sitting at the dining room table, feeling like an outsider, and not participating in the family scenario. All he could see was their profiles. He realized that his parents never looked at him and felt how much he wanted their attention. This yearning was a brand-new emotion to him, one that he felt very deeply. As he experienced it, he said, as if speaking to his parents, "Look at me. Pay attention to me." Alan cried even harder as he spoke these words.

For the first time, Alan experienced the connection he had never felt in life. By releasing the feelings associated with his early pain, his original need for attention was able to surface. If he had gotten the attention and love he needed from his parents, he would not have needed to protect himself from pain by separating himself from others. He would not have become an outsider, a nonparticipant in life. As Alan relived the scene in the dining room, he experienced every cell in his body tingling. His feelings were opening up and he was deluged with insights about how he kept everyone at a distance.

Note that the insights came *after* the release of the repressed feeling. You must first experience the full depth of your emotions if you are to gain any insights. It's much easier to intellectualize a feeling than experience it, because feeling an emotion often means reliving the old pain. Giving up control over your emotions, and relinquishing your defenses against them, can be scary. Once more you are subject to the same uncensored, unrestricted sensations you felt as a child. Too often people settle for simply understanding their feelings. But usually real change can only occur *after* the feelings are experienced. When repressed feelings are allowed to emerge, insights will inevitably follow. Since the person has experienced the pain he had been pushing down, he no longer needs to repress those feelings— and thus is able to confront the truth of his situation. Interestingly enough, the pain is often not as bad as the person imagines. Most people don't realize what a high price they've paid for repressing their feelings until they've experienced the freedom and relief that comes from lifting the lid on their blocked emotions.

Alan learned several things from opening himself up to his dream's message. One thing he discovered was that his mother was as guilty of ignoring him as his father. Both parents were too involved with themselves and each other to pay attention to Alan. This explained why Alan could not feel close to his mother, either.

Alan also found out why he avoided social situations and distanced himself from others. He unconsciously feared that everyone would treat him the way his parents did. Experience had also taught him to turn off his desires for attention. To a child, attention is the equivalent of love. That's why children who don't get positive attention often misbehave. Negative attention, in the form of scolding or even spanking, is preferable to no attention at all. By avoiding intimacy, Alan kept himself safe and out of pain. But his adaptations, which enabled him to survive childhood, isolated him as an adult. That, in turn, led to more pain. While he previously realized that his workaholic habits were a device to avoid painful social situations, he now understood that they were also a way to avoid intimacy with his wife.

Those insights profoundly changed his life. In the weeks that followed, Alan became clearer about his needs and desires, and expressed them more openly. He told his new law partners which projects he wanted to work on, instead of just blindly following their suggestions. His apathy turned into interest and involvement, and he was finally able to derive pleasure from his endeavors.

Alan also told his wife what he liked and didn't like in their relationship. This led to her sharing some of her unvoiced dissatisfactions. These discussions made them feel closer, and their original attraction to each other returned. Instead of avoiding each other, they looked for ways to spend more time together. They discovered that they enjoyed each other's company more than either could have imagined. Alan no longer tried to avoid arguments by automatically going along with whatever his wife wanted. Now he was willing to fight for his convictions when something was important to him. Far from being angry at no longer always getting her way, his wife greatly respected and appreciated her husband's new strength.

In the past, when Alan had to speak to people in social situations, he'd never talked about himself—his childhood had taught him that no one was interested in him. Thanks to his transformative dream, he now knew that speaking about himself was a bridge to other people, a way to connect with them. Since he understood that it was his parents who were lacking and not him, he was able to have dynamic, fulfilling conversations with others. Alan developed a keen sense of who listened to him and who didn't. When he spotted the latter he quickly headed in the other direction. In the past, he'd suffered through uncomfortable situations and allowed himself to be ignored, blaming himself for not being interesting. It was his habit to wait for others to address him. If no one did, he remained silent. Now he initiated conversations with people he didn't even know.

Alan consciously became assertive in all avenues of his life. His first big step was to bill clients immediately after completing their work, rather than waiting months or even a year to send an invoice.

Alan realized that his longtime apathy and passivity came from wanting to please others, just like he had wanted to please his father. Now he discovered that it wasn't fun to just do what others wanted. His hopeless search for his father's approval eased off and he focused his attention on what *he* liked to do. In the process he acquired a host of new interests, ranging from sailing to studying French. He found that these pursuits were much more rewarding than holing up in his office all day and night, just to prove to his father, who no longer existed, what a good son he was.

His relationship with me also changed. He no longer thought I was bored and uninterested. He didn't need my feedback or interpretations to feel enthusiastic about his life. Shortly after his transformation, he told me two dreams he had about me. In the first one, he looked out my office window at a beautiful view. This dream clearly illustrated his pleasure in seeing all the possibilities and options that lay ahead of him. In the other dream, we were on a raft together in the ocean. This suggested that he was on an exciting journey of discovery that would reveal who he was and how he felt about life. The ocean is a symbol for deep feelings, the unconscious, and rebirth.

Dreams are infallible barometers of our feelings. They accurately depict the atmosphere of our psyche. The Volvo in Alan's dream got right to the heart of his problem. It was the perfect symbol to represent the one time Alan felt his father might indeed love him. Once I understood its meaning, I could guide Alan back to where he needed to go.

Although discovering what a symbol personally means to us is the most rewarding kind of dream decoding, knowing the universal or general meaning of a dream symbol can provide clues that lead to the dream's message.

Symbols for Your Dream Dictionary:
Car: The id; virility; emblem of power and success.
View: Outlook on life.
Raft: Life preserver, bumpy travel, being adrift in the unconscious.

Alan's turning-point dream is about loss, a feeling that pervades the dreams of many people. Dreamers unconsciously use their life history, their repressed memories and unfulfilled wishes, and, some believe, their past lives to create a unique story that illustrates an important experience or feeling as precisely and powerfully as possible. Elderly people often report dreams of being lost, of walking in some unfamiliar place and not knowing where they are going. Depending on the individual, a dream of being lost can express any number of things. To one person, it could mean that his direction in life has become unclear. To another person, it might indicate that she is nearing the end of her journey on earth and is having difficulty facing the unknown that lies ahead of her.

Turning-point dreams can occur at any age. One young woman had a transformative dream a few months after her father's sudden death. The dreamer, only fourteen years old at the time, and her mother were left grief-stricken and destitute by this tragedy. The teenager dreamed that her father stood at the foot of her bed and said, "Everything is going to be okay." From that moment on, she felt optimistic about the future. Her depression and pessimism completely disappeared. As an adult, she learned that on that same night her mother was awakened by a noise. When her mother got out of bed and headed in the direction of the noise, she saw an apparition of her husband. Surprisingly, she was not afraid. The apparition told her, "Everything is going to be all right." Like her daughter, the dreamer's mother also felt instantly confident and hopeful. Here we have both a waking and a dreaming experience of a loved one returning from the dead to comfort his family. Such is the nature of dreams and experience!

Exercise: Give In to the Feelings You Awaken With
When you wake up in the morning with a strong feel-

ing (anger, depression, pleasure, and so on), surrender yourself completely to that emotion. It doesn't matter whether you understand the feeling or not. Give yourself an hour or so to fully experience your feeling, and follow it wherever it leads you. One way to do this is by writing from the feeling. Don't censor yourself or impose any direction on your thoughts and emotions— write whatever pops into your head, no matter how absurd or embarrassing it might seem. Give your unconscious free rein and let it guide you. The sooner you do this after awakening, the easier it will be to recapture the mood. You can also do this exercise by verbally exploring the feeling with a trusted mate or friend, someone to whom you can confide anything. Ask the listener not to interrupt you until you are finished.

You may wonder what this has to do with dreams. The answer is that your strong feeling is the residue from a dream you just had and then forgot. If you completely immerse yourself in this feeling, you can uncover the still-hidden emotions that are the clues to the dream's meaning. Another possibility is that the feeling might take you right to the buried memory that is responsible for your current mood. If that happens, you won't have to interpret the dream because you'll instantly *know* what it means.

A woman awoke one morning with a feeling of dread. She immediately wrote the following:

I'm supposed to see Tom this evening. I feel frightened. I'm not sure why. A familiar feeling. Will he stay overnight? I'm afraid of him. Or afraid of something. It's sort of a sick kind of fear. A feeling of discomfort, uncertainty. Maybe it comes from not knowing where my boundaries are. Losing my boundaries. Feeling fuzzy inside. Losing myself. Losing myself for him. Seeing him as sinister. Feeling I must do as he wishes, not as I wish. I swallow something. Maybe all of myself. I give him my power. Why do I submerge myself that way? I don't need to. I can be bold and assertive. It's like I'm overcompensating as hard as I can. I can set my boundaries.

The question "Shall he come home with me?" seems to scare me, as if I must let him make the decision. Why do I view him as so evil right now? I let myself be in his power. I become a mouse. It's as if I'm not allowed to assert myself. To not want what he wants. To want what he doesn't want. Maybe that's why I see him as evil, because I've given him full control of me. I've allowed myself to go emotionally limp.

This is a thing I do. Why? I always thought it had to do with giving up my will in my relationship with my mother. Trying on all those dresses she wanted me to wear when I was a child, then feeling icky and weird inside. The idea of pleasing. That sickening sweet idea.

When I was a child, the woman in the clothing store tried to please *me*. She was doing what I did. Seeing it in someone else, in her, filled me with disgust. She was so sweet to me. I felt these weird feelings toward her. I wanted to be rude and sadistic. I know now that I hated my need to please, but then I could only feel this anger toward someone else who did what I did. My therapist calls that "projecting." I wonder if other children acted the way I did with adults who fawn over them. Did they get the impulse to throw something in that smiling, adoring face? I think my sadism comes out toward Tom. Maybe I want to be mean rather than compliant. To say, "Hey, wait a minute. I don't want you to kiss me, because the idea of it makes me sick. Sick, like vomiting. The thought of kissing you makes me want to vomit."

I'd like to say, "Don't fawn over me," to the woman in the clothing store. "What are you fawning for anyway? Do you really think I'm adorable or are you pretending so that you can make a sale? Are you trying to please my mother?"

God, I'm disgusting when I go along with something I don't like. Suppose I say to Tom, "It's been a long time since I've done this. You're going further and faster than I want to go. I'm not ready for it. Why should I take off my clothes with you just because *you* want it? Why should I be attracted to you just because you're attracted to me?"

After the woman wrote this, she felt much clearer about what was really going on. Her feeling of dread disappeared and she vowed to be honest with Tom. She got in touch with some of her attitudes toward Tom that she hadn't been able to identify before: her anger at him for expecting her to be there whenever he wanted her, her frustration over the way he never paid attention to what she needed, her resentment over his indifference when she asked for something she wanted. Tom wanted to call all the shots, she concluded. She decided not to let him do that anymore. By discovering her initial, childhood experiences of substituting her genuine feelings with false ones, it became clear to her that she was trained at an early age to pretend to feel things she didn't really feel and to submit to the wishes of others instead of pursuing her own desires.

The message this woman learned was invaluable. Forced to look at the way she cheated herself, she altered her whole approach to relationships with other people. She carefully examined her attitudes, assumptions, and behavior patterns—and discarded all the ones that undermined and sabotaged the satisfaction and fulfillment she was determined to have in her life. At the same time, she was able to clearly identify her new standards and take the necessary actions to implement them. Delving into the feelings she had awakened with, feelings that no doubt stemmed from a forgotten dream the night before, enabled her to make the concrete, fundamental changes required to substantially improve her life.

SEVEN

The Monster in
the Closet

An architect, whom I shall call Marcy, wanted to start her own business and needed to find office space. During her search, she had a horrifying nightmare. It haunted her until she told it to her primal therapy group. After relaying the dream to her group, she went into the adjoining padded, soundproofed primal room and gave in to the feelings of her dream. In less than an hour, Marcy came out of the room and triumphantly announced that she knew what the dream meant. This is remarkable when you consider that it may take weeks, months, or even years for a person to fully understand a dream. This was her dream:

DREAM: *While looking for office space I enter a loft. I instantly know that it's perfect for my new business. As I leave, I notice a door next to the exit door. I open that door and see a tall, naked man with big bulging eyes who's covered with bruises. His skin is so white it looks like the blood has been drained from his body. Obviously dead, he's hanging from the door. He reminds me of the zombies and mummies I saw in the movies when I was a kid. I'm so terrified that I wake up from the dream.*

When Marcy exited the primal room, she informed the group of the dream's important message. "I know who the dead man is. He's my f—— father, the one who's standing in my way."

How did she come to that realization? Why was this dream so important, a turning point in her life?

Marcy explained what was happening in her life at the time of the dream. Naturally, this information is vital to understanding the meaning of a dream. Marcy was nervous about opening her own business. She feared that it would overwhelm her and doubted she could do everything that had to be done. During that period she envisioned herself as paralyzed a lot of the time. "It's my damage," she said, "my old stuff." She was especially worried about how a *woman* handles her own business.

It had not initially occurred to Marcy to bring this dream to her primal therapy group. In fact, this was the first time she had mentioned a dream in group. But the dream had haunted her all day long, and she had awakened that morning with an uneasy feeling in the pit of her stomach. When a dream stays with someone for a day or so, it is a sure sign that dream has something important to say. The image of the pale dead man with big bulging eyes had stayed in Marcy's mind because it was so frightening. When she first saw him in her dream she did not realize he was naked. And it was only after she noticed his nakedness that she knew he was dead. Marcy knew from past experience that the only way to free herself from thinking about a disturbing dream symbol was to allow herself to confront it. People often suppress or cut off disturbing thoughts and feelings in an effort to get rid of them. Unfortunately that technique doesn't work—the unresolved material continues to pop up again and again in one form or another.

Marcy's technique was a very effective approach, because once we meet the demon face-to-face, it loses its hold on us.

"I was determined to discover what this dream meant," Marcy explained, "and I'm convinced that's why I was able to figure it out. I knew it was significant. And I was *willing* to know its message—which means that I was willing to jump over whatever fear there was. I asked myself, 'What is the feeling in the dream?' That's the only way for me to get at what's really going on inside. Instead of running away from this stuff, I allowed myself to sink into it. It's hard to verbalize this process. So much of it is just feeling what comes up for you."

At the time of the dream, Marcy knew she had major stumbling blocks about moving into her own office. She had been working out of her home for two years; it felt like a safe haven. But she also knew she had to get out into the world. She was terrified, but wasn't exactly sure what she was terrified of. There was terror both in her life and in the dream. When a feeling in life matches the one in the dream, we have a definite clue to the dream's meaning.

At the beginning of the dream, Marcy felt excited and elated about the space she was looking at. She thought she had found the perfect place for her office. It was a big open area, the paneling was light-colored, and the feeling was homey, light, and happy. But then, as she was getting ready to leave, she noticed the door next to the exit door. She opened it up, and there was the dead man with the big bulging eyes hanging from the door. Marcy didn't remember if she screamed. But she did remember letting out "this incredible gasp of terror, absolute terror."

Marcy's dream depicted a universal situation. The

dreamer created in her dream the very thing she wanted, but then introduced a disturbing element that prevented her from getting it. This resembles the Freudian wish-fulfillment dream that turns into a nightmare. According to Freudian dream interpretation, Marcy's dream expressed a forbidden wish that was intolerable to her superego because of its incestuous implications. She therefore squelched the wish by turning her dream into a nightmare. Although the theory might be partially true, there's a good chance that it overlooks the most important meaning. That is one of the dangers of using theory to interpret dreams. I believe there is no better dream expert than the dreamer herself. She created the dream, albeit unconsciously, and thus is in the best position to discern its meaning. Through consciously reexperiencing her feelings in the dream, Marcy was able to unravel its meaning. When we get to that meaning, you will see that it disagrees with the Freudian interpretation above.

At the point in the dream that Marcy realized the man was dead, she recalled thinking, "Should I do something about this? Should I help him?" But her terror was so intense that she pulled herself out of the dream instead. Most people, in fact, wake themselves up to escape from the terror of a nightmare. That makes a lot of sense, since dream symbols are meant to conceal unbearably painful feelings. During our waking life we have our defenses to protect us from pain and discomfort, and during our sleep we have our dreams. The only difference is that if we are willing to look, we can discover the truth in our dreams. Freud regarded nightmares as libidinal wishes (sexual or aggressive) that are so powerful they break through the dreamer's censorship.

Nightmares can teach us so much. The intensity of

fear indicates an issue of life-or-death importance to the dreamer. Nightmares can be transformative dreams, providing we are willing to face our fears. Dreams provide a safe arena for this.

Marcy was convinced that the terror of her dream stayed with her all day because she pulled herself out of it by waking up. Since she couldn't get rid of her fear, she finally said to herself: "Okay, I want an answer, I want to know what this is about." She went into the primal room and immediately immersed herself in her feelings, which were right at the surface.

I asked Marcy to describe what it was like to get into her feelings. "It's hard to describe," she said. "For me, it's just allowing whatever fear, whatever pain there is to engulf me. Not to cut it off. It's a physical thing. When I do cut off my feelings, I literally feel it in my gut or around my solar plexus. I feel myself trying to physically bear down to cut off the feeling. But I don't do it. Instead I let out whatever is there. I let myself hit the pillows. I let myself cry. I let myself feel like a baby, which is what it sometimes feels like. In this case, I needed to yell, so I did. I needed to pound pillows, so I let myself do it. And at some point, I just opened up. The only way I can describe it is to say that the feeling that I had been carrying around all day from having that dream suddenly dissipated. The light came shining through. In that moment I realized that the dead man was my father. It was the spector of my father standing in my way of being an adult, of being a professional, of being out in the world."

How was Marcy's father standing in her way? I asked. Marcy explained that while growing up, her father took care of everything. Since he handled everything, she was not responsible for anything. If she dared to think that she should take care of something, she'd be usurping his role. She came out of the primal room angry at her father, but her anger really had nothing to do with how she felt about her father now. They had resolved the bad feelings between them before he died.

The dream, however, revealed that Marcy had not forgotten her conflicts with her father. The two of them had made peace, had even acknowledged a deep, loving relationship based on trust. Yet as a child, Marcy never expressed the anger, hurt, and fear she harbored toward him. These unexpressed feelings lingered on, as they do in all of us until we deal with them.

Her father was lord of the household, king of their patriarchal home. Her mother was a teacher and went back to work part-time when Marcy was ten. In retrospect, Marcy didn't know how her mother managed. She did everything *and* worked besides. All her father had to do was work. By the time he came home, her mother had cooked dinner, cleaned the house, picked up the dry cleaning, and done the laundry. His after-work chores consisted of drinking two cocktails. Sometimes he brought work home from the office, but he never worked on it.

Even though Marcy grew up in a male-dominated house, she was expected to have a career. She was extremely bright and was always at the top of her class. Everyone expected her to go to college, which she did. However, she never worked very hard in college. In fact, she felt she got away with murder. She waited till the last minute to do her homework and still got A's. Not once did she receive anything less than a B. She worked hard only when absolutely necessary.

When Marcy discovered that the dead man in her dream was her father, she realized the dream was about what she called "the male-female thing." Both her mother and her aunt were primarily housewives. Her mother's best friend was an ophthalmologist. She was Marcy's main role model of a working woman. Marcy adored her and thought she was an extraordinary woman. Marcy was not aware of how much these ideas about male superiority were ingrained in her. "Even though I told myself I was as smart as any man, I didn't believe I could do what they did. When I got out of school I admired the men who went off and started their own businesses. I thought to myself, How can they do that? What makes them think they can succeed? I never thought I could do something like that. There was no way that I could just go off and start my own business like them."

When Marcy realized this was a dream about her father, several things became clear to her. While she appreciated that her father always took care of everything for her, she saw that she also longed for independence and competence like his. Marcy wondered if she felt that she couldn't compete with men. Until she discovered the meaning of this dream, she had never been aware that she unconsciously felt at a disadvantage. She realized that deep down she believed she couldn't open up an office and be a success because she was "a girl." She was ashamed of that thought because she had always consciously felt that women were as good as, if not better than, men. During her relationships with men she had noticed they seemed to be in competition with her. She believed they thought they had to outdo her because she was so smart—not book smart, she explained, but perceptive, intuitive, and full of common sense.

The most important thing about the dream, Marcy realized, was that it brought out her anger with her father, an anger she had long suppressed. At first she thought that her anger was self-manufactured, an imaginary block that she had put up. She was not really angry at *him*, she reasoned, but at what she had projected *onto* him. She was sure she was unfairly blaming him because she couldn't go forward in the world, when it had nothing to do with him.

However, as Marcy continued to speak about her father, it became apparent that some of her anger toward him was indeed well founded. At first she didn't want to admit it. She preferred to blame herself, as children are wont to do. Children protect the parent because they are afraid their anger will drive away the parent, whom they desperately need. More than anything, children want the parent to keep on loving them. Gradually Marcy verbalized her anger.

One problem was that her father and she were very much alike, Marcy said. She admitted that she was angry at her father because, in retrospect, she saw that he dumped a lot of his anger on her. Nevertheless she adored him. As a child, she loved to be with him. They played baseball and tennis, did a lot of things together. When Marcy became an adolescent, it seemed he couldn't deal with the idea that she'd soon be a woman. He was often sarcastic, mean, and insensitive. She felt that he pushed her away and there was nothing she could do about it. She retaliated by refusing to play tennis with him, since he loved the game. During this period Marcy also had difficulties with her mother, who was abusive to her. In Marcy's mind, the two of them were pitted against her.

Marcy's mother was both physically and verbally abusive and destroyed Marcy's will and self-esteem. The result was that Marcy was in constant anguish. Feeling unloved and rejected, Marcy didn't want to be alive. She asked herself, "How can I live if nobody likes me?" The pain from feeling hated by her mother and mistreated by her father were still inside Marcy when she had the dream. By being aware of this pain, she had an excellent chance of working it through.

Dream characters also represent unrecognized aspects of the dreamer. In this case, Marcy's father's body was covered with bruises. Why she dreamed of him this way will come out later. Working on the dream, she realized that the bruises were not only her father's but her own.

By releasing her dream feelings, Marcy was able to discover that the frightening man in her dream was her father. But something else also pointed in that direction. She said that the man in the dream was dead. The word "dead" is very close to the word "Dad." Dreams are notorious for using puns. Words that sound like the actual thing the dream symbol represents give a clue to its meaning. "Dad" was a person who was no longer alive in the material world but lived on inside of Marcy.

Here's another example of how similarities in words reveal the dream's hidden meaning: A woman kept dreaming of moths, until she figured out that she was really dreaming of mother. The word "moth" is the root of "mother." This woman often wrote down her dreams, abbreviating "mother" to "moth." Her mother appeared in her dream as a moth who kept dive-bombing her until she swatted it away.

Marcy's father had died three years before, and those three years were very significant in Marcy's development. She speculated that if her father hadn't died, she would still be paralyzed. Her father's death forced her to be an adult. He was the one who had taken care of everything. With him gone, Marcy had to fill that role herself, which gave her the opportunity to become her own person.

Her first act was to change careers. She had been a musician for many years, but wasn't getting anywhere with it. Marcy also had a natural gift for design. It dawned on her that she could find her niche in a field that had always fascinated her: architecture. When she made the big decision to change careers, she said "the lights went on," and she knew it was the absolutely right thing to do. No matter what happened in the future, she would always be able to find work as an architect, whereas the streets swarmed with unemployed musicians. She also knew that having her own business would give her control and power.

Marcy had just gotten a divorce when she began going to architecture school, near her parents' home. She spent weeknights at her parents' house, and felt she had to let go of all her anger and stop acting like a frustrated little kid. Putting aside her resentment improved her relationship with her mother in some ways. It worked even better with her father, until he died. She shared things with them, which she had never done before. Previously, she never shared any news about her life with them because she had regarded them as the enemy since she was an adolescent. Marcy saw during that period that there had to be give and take between her and her parents. If she wanted to receive something from them she had to give something back.

Marcy admired her father for working his way up in his profession. Nobody gave him anything. But she also saw that he was the prototypical sexist male. She remembered how, as a teenager, she heard his disgust at having to hire women in his office. He didn't want to have to deal with women employees, because he thought they were too emotional. He resented women in the office. Marcy got angry at the time, and now, years later, she looked back on that incident and thought, How dare he say this to his seventeen-year-old daughter! His prejudice toward women tied into the dream symbol of her father standing in the door, standing in the way of her achieving something.

Marcy allowed that he eventually outgrew his chauvinistic attitudes toward women. He mellowed out when he had cancer—it really changed his way of thinking. By the time he died, he and Marcy had become very close. Marcy talked to him about a lot of things that she never shared with her mother, like Buddhism. She gave her father some exercises to do and bought him books by the Dalai Lama that gave him inner peace. By the time he died, she was confident that he absolutely adored her and was proud of her. Marcy cherished that and tried to think of that instead of all the hurtful things he'd done when she was a young, unsure teenager.

In further reflecting on her dream, Marcy wondered why she dreamed of her father as a bruised zombie. She realized her childhood fear of him made her have dreams of being chased by a monster. That monster looked like the zombies and mummies in the old 1950s' horror movies. The monster painstakingly chased her at an excruciatingly slow pace. Marcy found it interesting that she dreamed of the monster as a man. Her mother was more abusive, but her father had a meaner temper. Even though she always thought of her mother as the worse of the two, it was a man that she was afraid might attack her.

"I used to have nightmares when I was a child—of something dead, something ugly and disgusting and festering. Something really gross. Maybe in some ways it represented myself, being bruised and beaten up. That's finished, that's done with. But I also link it to my father in another way, because my father was kind of beaten up . . . in an unfair way. He was a very vibrant, exciting, physical man, and his physicality was taken away from him by the bone cancer—he lost his muscle control. I knew my father could never live in a wheelchair, and indeed he died before he ever had to use one. But it was such agony to watch him walk so laboriously during the year or so before he died. I totally freaked out when I saw him swaying as he walked, with his fists clenched and his arms held a certain way. Everything was such an effort for him. Then I flashed back to when he was angry. He had a terrible, terrible temper. He sometimes looked like he was holding his anger back, holding it all in. The cancer looked like a manifestation of what he used to be like. It was like he made his anger physical. For him the anger was his cancer.

"I have this one recurring memory—it hasn't come up for a long time—about when I was less than eight years old. I remember being afraid of my father. It was a Sunday twilight afternoon in winter, about four o'clock. I see me standing and my father walking toward me. I'm terrified. But I don't remember what it was about, except that he probably hit me to discipline me. But I don't yet have a complete picture about my terror of my father.

"I think the dream is saying that my father is dead and my childhood terror of him is finished, gone. My old fear is dead and gone, and I need to close the door behind me and go on. In fact, it's really what I did after the dream."

Despite her words, Marcy was not completely convinced that her fear was gone, and neither was I. If the dream was trying to tell her that her fear was over, she would not have had to wake herself up from her nightmare. She would have conquered the fear or walked away from it in her dream. The interpretation she gives above is only partially correct. Her thoughts that followed contain another piece of the puzzle. "It's so hard to let go of what was so horrible. When you've been abused, you hold on to it. It has something to do with wanting your parents' approval, no matter how terrible they might have been."

The message in Marcy's dream that empowered her was the sign to close the door, because that's what she actually did after the dream. She bought her own loft and opened up her own practice. She got a lot of clients and her business was successful. The dream was a turning point in her life. It gave her direction about what she had to do. She had wanted to open an office for a while, but had resisted. The dream showed her what her resistance was: fear of moving forward in her life and achieving what she knew she could achieve.

Marcy still works on the fear and guilt associated with her father. The turning-point message of her dream was that she did not have to let him stand in the way of her success. Despite some still unresolved feelings, this message freed her to take an action. That action changed her life.

The key to Marcy's success was facing the terror in her dream while she was awake. By surrendering to her feelings, the message of her dream revealed itself. Interestingly, confronting fears in a dream was an alleged practice among the Senoi aboriginies of Malaysia. From the time they could speak, they were taught to tell their dreams the next morning, and were instructed to face their dream fears directly. This practice shaped them into people who were not only fearless in life, but loving as well. Love flourishes best when fear is absent.

Marcy's dream is proof that when we have the courage to surrender to our feelings and look our demons in the eye, we can then acquire what we want in life. The monster in the closet is like the skeleton in the closet. We must open that closed door and confront the monster if we are to grow. Only then can we close the door on the fear, guilt, and pain that keeps us paralyzed and frightened. What most people don't realize is that avoiding their feelings hurts a lot more than accepting them.

It is significant that Marcy dreamed about a monster in a closet. That image is common in children who are four and five years old. Children that age often fear the dark because they think that monsters are hiding in the closet and dragons are lurking under the bed. The supernatural is real to them, and they fear all sorts of bogeymen, ghosts, and witches. Bruno Bettleheim, in his classic book *The Uses of Enchantment*, explains that since the child's "rationality has as yet poor control over his unconscious, the child's imagination runs away with him under the pressure of his emotions and unsolved conflicts. A child's barely emerging ability to reason is soon overwhelmed by anxieties, hopes, fears, desires, loves, and hates—which become woven into whatever the child began thinking about." Marcy's dream about her father brought back the fears she experienced at that young age. By continuing to release her feelings about this frightening image, she will eventually discover the whole truth about her fear.

Symbols for Your Dream Dictionary:
Loft: Self, lofty, high.
Bruises: Imperfections.
Exit door: A way out, death, escape.
Naked: The real person, beneath the facade, vulnerability.
Dead man: A person we feel hostile toward.

Exercise: Go Back into the Dream

Marcy explained how to access feelings in this chapter. Of course she's had a lot of practice at this due to her involvement in primal therapy. Some people are close to their feelings and can reach them easily. If you are one of those people, just do what Marcy did. Find a place where it's safe to scream or cry or yell, where there will be no interference. Lie down in a comfortable position, preferably on a mat. Allow the dream to come back into your mind. Be guided by the feelings you had in the dream. For Marcy, it was the terror of seeing the dead man hanging from the door. If you had no specific feelings, let yourself relax, and ask yourself these questions:

What am I feeling now?

Do I have any particular physical tensions or sensations?

Can I allow myself to experience what they are? (Try focusing your mind on the tensions or sensations in your body and breathe into them.)

Am I having any associations or memories right now?

Was there an earlier time in my life, such as my childhood, when I felt this way?

What are the details of that situation? Who comes into my mind?

What would I say about my feelings to the person or persons who triggered these emotions?

Where are my feelings leading me? Can I go with them?

Can I let myself express them?

Marcy allowed herself to be very sensitive to every nuance of her sensations and feelings. She did not resist, and she permitted herself to go where her emotions led her. She knew that no harm would come to her, even though she surrendered herself to her terror. If you are resistant to doing this, don't force it. It will happen

when you are ready. The most important thing is to relax your mind and body as much as possible. Give your
thoughts and feelings the time and space to emerge.
Tension is a way of keeping your feelings at bay. We
experience our emotions throughout our bodies—in our
necks, backs, and stomachs, for example. Locate the
parts of your body that feel tight and rigid; concentrate
on relaxing them. As you relax, your emotions will rise
to the surface.

EIGHT

Under the Boardwalk

The following dream was a turning point in this patient's therapy and life. Jan didn't suspect that she had been sexually violated by her father until she was in her early forties. She entered therapy to recall key memories and work through them. Her father was a brutal man in many ways, but Jan had no memory of sexual abuse. She clearly recalled his verbal abuse, though, in the form of bullying, derogatory comments, and mockery.

DREAM: *I'm lying in my bed in the house where I grew up. I hear my father walk into my room and sense him standing behind me. He puts his index finger in my mouth and presses it on my gums as he outlines the entire rim of my mouth. I pretend to be asleep, but I'm intensely aware of what is going on. I lie on my left side and he puts his left hand under my left breast. He presses me into his hand by pushing my back with his other hand. This takes only a few seconds. I am aware of his every movement. I try to photograph it in my mind so I can bring it in to my therapist as evidence of his transgression. He quickly leaves. When I awaken I am astounded that this wa, only a dream; it was so vivid I could swear it reall happened.*

Was this the dream that Jan had come into therapy to have? Some of her previous dreams had intimated incest, but none as blatantly as this one. Her mother had recently told her things about her father that further suggested incest. She wanted to have an actual memory of her father molesting her, so she could be sure it happened. Until she had proof she did not feel entitled to be angry at him or to blame him for the failures in her life. Incest could explain why she was so angry with the men with whom she had become involved. She felt that men hated her, too. Jan blamed herself for her two failed marriages. In short, whenever she was angry at a man, she felt there was something wrong with her. As a result, she hated herself. This dream occurred after one and a half years of therapy.

Her father had always been a violent man. He alternated between struggling to control his anger and letting it loose on whomever was around. She remembered him slapping her mother and beating up her brothers during his uncontrollable rages. When he got angry, the rest of the family froze. Her father looked like a madman during his rages. His eyes bulged, drool rolled down the sides of his mouth, and the veins protruded in his head. He smashed dishes and threw bottles. Most frightening, his rage always seemed to come without warning. Jan remembered the time he thought her brother had used a disrespectful tone of voice. He picked the boy up off the living room floor and beat him till he was a motionless heap in the corner. Anything could set her father and nothing could stop him. Later he would be with remorse, not because he had hurt someone cause he had lost control.

felt trapped by him. He teased her to the point she had no recourse but to scream at him. At he purposely provoked him until he reached the boiling point. She hated him and yet felt compelled to bring about what she most feared—an angry explosion. It was her way of getting some control over the situation. She preferred to believe she provoked his anger rather than face the possibility that he basically didn't love her and truly wanted to kill her. This realization of why she provoked him came out in the course of therapy. Until then she believed that she deserved his rage.

When her father was in a good mood, he teased her, mocked her, and insinuated that she was stupid. He never agreed with her about anything. He often commented that no man would want her because she was so contentious. He took great joy in humiliating her.

Shortly before she entered therapy, Jan's mother told her that her father had kissed Jan on the lips when she was three years old, and had also touched her genitals. Jan did not know whether she could trust her mother's perceptions, because her mother lived so much in her own world. Her mother protected neither herself nor her children from her husband's violence. Jan did, however, wonder why she was the one member of the family who had remained physically unharmed by him. She questioned whether her constant discomfort around her father, especially when he was in a playful mood, had anything to do with his sexual feelings toward her. Jan tightened up and felt uncomfortable in his presence. Some of her discomfort stemmed from his violence and his taunting, but she wondered if that was the whole picture.

Jan had had other dreams that suggested her father abused her sexually. These dreams were more symbolic. As she got closer to her feelings in therapy, her dreams became more realistic. As people get deeper into their feelings, their dreams tend to become less symbolic— because it is not as necessary to disguise their meaning.

In a prior dream, Jan was walking near a wall underneath the boardwalk in Atlantic City. It was dark. Huge, hard, devouring waves kept getting higher and higher. She was afraid she was going to be swept away. The waves crashed down on her and pushed her against a wall. She was shoved up against her father's bureau drawer. She felt something brush against her left thigh. She picked the object up and was horrified. It was a Barbie doll with dark hair. The doll had missing limbs, as if it were a dead body. Jan kept saying to herself, "This is a dead body." When she came out from underneath the boardwalk, the water was calm and it was light outside. A woman was sitting at a card table, her back to the ocean, where the water broke onto the sand. The dreamer reported to the woman that a body had been found. She was deeply upset.

Jan told me this dream early in therapy. The dreams related in the first sessions of therapy are extremely important. Although the dream about her father coming into the room was her turning-point dream, this dream of being knocked against her father's bureau further suggested that he had inflicted deep damage upon her.

The dream also contained symbolism frequently observed in the dreams of people who have repressed their memories of sexual abuse. One of those symbols was the doll. A doll is a representation of a child, but the doll is not a real child. It is the dead child, the child whose feelings are numb. A child who has been sexually molested often represses anger at this assault on the self. The anger is repressed partly out of denial of the horror that has taken place and partly out of the child's need to survive. One reason the memories of childhood sexual molestation become buried is that the molesters often threaten to kill the children if they tell. Sexual abuse causes great confusion in a child because the child wants to believe her parent is a good parent, yet she knows this behavior is anything but good. The child desperately needs to be loved and protected by a parent, and may sacrifice her own psychic health to maintain, as in this case, the illusion of love. The symbol of the doll in the dream represents the dead child. The child literally deadens herself psychologically as a way to keep on living.

Jan said that the doll felt like a baby in the dream. She elaborated, "In this dream, I feel I've found not the inner child, but a dead body."

Missing limbs are common symbols in the dreams of people who have survived childhood sexual molestation. Imagine dreaming that parts of your body are missing! Incest shatters the sense of self. Throughout his lifetime, the person feels he can no longer set his own boundaries. Anyone has access now, and there is no protection against this. Incest survivors feel confused. How can they still love the adult, whom they need, when this same adult had inflicted such pain upon them? Therapy is one way to reverse this tragedy.

The missing limbs also suggest the victim's helplessness and refusal to fight back; without limbs there is no fight. The sexual molestation renders the child defenseless, and brings on a state of terror. There is fear both of her assailant as well as of her own wish to kill her assailant. All feelings of self-worth have been destroyed.

To make matters worse, the little girl who has been molested by her father feels guilt over having been chosen over Mommy as a sexual partner. The same is true of the little boy who's been molested by his mother. The relationship to the benign parent, therefore, is also marred. When Jan told me this dream, she said I represented the woman in the dream sitting with her back to the ocean. By reporting the body to me, she is symbolically telling me what her father has done to her. I am seen as the one who can possibly punish and stop her father, for at the time of the suspected molestation there was no one she could tell.

Jan had other associations to this dream as well. In the dream, Jan was thrown against her father's bureau drawer by the "huge, hard, devouring waves." The waves represent powerful feelings. No one was allowed near her father's bureau drawer, she told me. It was private, and perhaps even secret. Yet in the dream it is Jan who was thrown up against it, so that she was privy to this secret knowledge. This was a further suggestion that incest did take place.

Jan said that Atlantic City was the family's summer vacation spot when she was three or four. Her father came on weekends, and swam at dusk. Thus, the dream establishes the age at which the molestation took place, if indeed it occurred, and the possible time of day: dusk. But until a waking memory of the actual event is produced, a dream such as this indicates only a possibility, not a fact. Its value lies in helping the dreamer explore all the feelings associated with the dream.

As we continued to work together, more details about Jan's relationship with her father emerged. He particularly liked to arouse excitement in his children, only to follow it up with disappointment. Jan's mother always made excuses for him and said he was only playing. At Christmastime, when the children woke up early to unwrap the presents under the tree, he took particular delight in watching them unwrap presents that were not presents at all—for example, kitchen utensils or pieces of fruit. He wrapped these objects like gifts to fool them—and laughed out loud when their excitement turned to disappointment.

When Jan was seven she found a kitten. Her mother told her she could keep it outdoors. Jan fed it and took care of it. One day when her parents weren't home, she brought the kitten into the house. It hid in her father's den, and she couldn't retrieve it. Her father came home in an angry mood, and, upon hearing about the kitten, arbitrarily decided that the kitten was responsible for a spot he noticed on the carpet. He slammed the door of his den, leaving Jan outside. Shouting with rage, he searched for the kitten by violently lifting up furniture and then dropping it. Jan frantically worried that the kitten would be smashed or stomped to death in the process. She stood outside the door of the den with her mother and screamed, "He's going to kill the kitten!" Her voice was high-pitched and shrill. Her mother reprimanded her for being hysterical. Jan had never shown such terror in the past. Fear was something she used all her defenses against feeling, let alone showing. Jan felt helpless. Finally the door swung open and a tiny ball of fur came shooting out. The kitten had not been killed, but could easily have died of fright.

In telling me this story, Jan realized that this was one of the only memories she had of fearing her father. Her heart pounded when he went out of control, but she experienced that as more of a body sensation than the emotion of fear. She had been terrified on other occasions in her life, but confessed that she always felt like she was overreacting. It wasn't until she told me about the kitten that she connected fear with her father. It would have been too dangerous for her to let herself know how frightened she really was. The incident with the kitten caught her off-guard. The kitten, of course, was a projection of herself. She feared for the kitten's life just as she feared for her own. Before that incident,

Jan had felt only anger, and not fear, at the fact that her father was so hostile toward her.

Returning to her turning-point dream: her father molesting her in her room only made sense when she reenacted it. I asked her to get into the position she was in in her dream. She lay down with her back to me and imagined herself in her childhood bedroom in Philadelphia. "Let yourself go back into the dream," I said. "What's coming up for you?"

She replied, "I'm aware of him coming into the room and standing behind me. I can even imagine him from the back, his broad, muscular shoulders, his thinning hair. I see him doing to me all the things I experienced but couldn't see at the time because I was pretending to be asleep. As I see him molest me, I feel angry. He thinks I am asleep. He's sneaky. I never understood that before as vividly as I do now. I despise him. It's grotesque, his putting his index finger in my mouth and pressing down hard. I know that sounds sexual." (The symbols and actions in Jan's dream are, of course, sexual: the bed; Jan in the bed and her father standing behind her; the index finger in her mouth, which represents a phallic object inside of her; and Jan's father pressing her breast into his hand. In addition, childhood sexual molestation is implied by the setting: Jan's childhood bedroom.)

As Jan acknowledged her father's perversion, she understood why she'd never trusted him. He'd gotten a lascivious charge from doing seemingly harmless things to her. More childhood memories bubbled up. "I remember how he played with me when I was a child. He liked to poke and jab me in so-called fun. I hated it. When I told him to stop, he'd become angry and threatening. No one was around to tell him to stop. My mother didn't stop it. I felt she knew what was going on, but she never intervened. I had no protection from him.

"My father bought me a pair of boxing gloves and insisted on boxing with me. He never did that with my brothers, just with me. I hated it, but he made me do it. Sometimes I got so angry at his incessant poking that I hit him as hard as I could. Other times I screamed 'stop,' but he never did. Instead he used my protest as his rationale for getting even madder. He sadistically punched me while preventing me from punching him back. I couldn't show any fear or anger, because that ignited his cruel rage. I realize now that boxing with me was just his sneaky way of touching me. Now I understand why I felt so angry at him and so uncomfortable in his presence. I think of him as sick—really, really sick. I never wanted to engage in this so-called play. He always initiated it, and if I didn't respond, he just kept punching me until I finally punched him back. He made me so angry that I wanted to punch him. He pulled me into this sick game, and I was totally at his mercy. I realize now that it's important for me to see myself as a helpless victim, and to view my father as a cruel man who acted out his mental illness with an innocent child.

"I also realize that I pretended to be asleep in the dream so I could catch him in the act without him knowing. Confronting him was too dangerous. He would have denied everything—and it would have led to a terrible fight that I would lose. I was also afraid of my mother finding out. I didn't know what she would do. Would she withdraw, as she so often did? Or would she become indignant and leave him? Or maybe she would blame me. If I brought it out in the open, I was sure the family would fall apart. Either that or my mother would just continue to do what she had always done, put up with it and feel trapped. She was so dependent on him that she probably would have just accepted it and suffered in silence. I was also scared that if I accused my father of molesting me, it might make him even more violent.

"In the dream, I wanted to catch him in the act, so I could report it to my therapist and work out my problems about it. Perhaps then I could get free somehow, free to know that all men are not like my father. Free to know that I'm not hateful, even though my father acted hatefully toward me. Free to go on with my life, and leave all the rage, fear, and distrust behind."

Jan said she was disappointed and confused when she woke up and realized the bedroom molestation was only a dream. She wondered if the scene in her bedroom ever took place, and despaired that she might never know for certain. She also wondered if she dreamed it because she wanted to believe her father molested her. "Even if that's true," she asked herself, "does that invalidate my feelings about him?" She realized the answer was no. "I know that he really was a sneaky, sick, hateful man. It's a big weight off my shoulders to know I didn't bring this upon myself."

Although it would have confirmed her suspicions if she'd discovered that her father had actually violated her, it was clear that his sadistic fondness for touching her was a form of sexual molestation. The effects of this kind of sexual behavior can be as psychologically damaging as actual physical penetration. In both cases, the end result is confusion over personal boundaries, fragmentation of self, loss of trust, unexplained terror and rage, and a deep sense of shame. What could be more heinous than crippling one's own flesh and blood in this way!

As Jan worked through the feelings of rage, terror, and hatred evoked by her dream, she felt a new sense of self. She began to like herself. Her sense of boundaries became stronger. Strangely enough, working through her negative feelings toward her father enabled her buried need for him to emerge. Although she discovered how truly sick he really was, she also uncovered a childhood longing for him that predated his abuse. Allowing herself to feel this early need for a loving, protective father connected her to the love inside herself. This dream provided the key that enabled Jan to undo the confusion from her childhood, understand her discomfort toward her father, and let go of the hate directed at herself.

One of the tragic wounds of incest is the loss of trust of other human beings. Without trust it is impossible to love. The victim is often crippled for life, unable to have lasting relationships or make commitments.

My patient Jim had a dream about incest that frightened him so deeply he refused to believe it happened. Hopefully this denial is temporary, because his dream is an invaluable gift that could show him the source of his current misery. His company relocated him to Chicago, so he did not stay in therapy long enough to assimilate the truth contained in the dream. I include it here, however, for several reasons: (1) the dream's symbolism; (2) the traumatic event uncovered by this dream, which could have remained secret for his entire life; and (3) the illustration of how fear can prevent a dreamer from processing a dream that could lead the way to inner freedom. This was a transformative dream, but the dreamer was too frightened to confront the painful feelings associated with the implied event. If he had been able to continue therapy, I would have helped him work through these feelings.

Hopefully Jim has had other similar dreams since

then or has acquired the determination and strength to take another look at this dream's message. Though dream messages can seem frightening, people rarely dream about things they're not ready to deal with. If something is too painful or overwhelming, the dream is either forgotten or it never occurs. This was Jim's dream:

DREAM: *I walk down a street in my childhood neighborhood. Although I don't recognize it, it seems to be on the outskirts of town. I come to a big open space, which is used as a dump. I see heaps of human body parts—dismembered arms, legs, torsos, and heads—piled up on top of each other. There are thousands of maggots and rats among the rotting bodies. The scene is horrible and depressing. Terrified, I run to tell people what I saw. No one believes me. I plead with them, and finally some men come with me to witness this grotesque sight. When we arrive at the dump there's nothing there. All the bodies are gone. The men laugh at me. I am dumbfounded. We all leave. Later I return to the dump to check again. Once more I see piles of broken bodies. It is the worst nightmare of my life.*

Jim was so distraught over this dream that he called me the next morning. He felt that he couldn't wait until our scheduled session to tell me about it.

When we met again, we worked on the dream together. I asked him to relax, close his eyes, and take three deep breaths. When he was ready, I told him to enter the dream at any part he wanted. In a strangled voice, he said, "I'm looking at the dump." He looked horrified as he whispered, "I think my father molested me." He sobbed uncontrollably as he said in broken gasps, "That couldn't be true. Could it?" He clearly hoped that I would reassure him that it couldn't. "Could it be true?" he repeated. I couldn't give him the answer he wanted because his response suggested a truth he didn't want to know. When emotions are that strong, they can lead to buried information the conscious mind has blocked. Jim ended up with a sense of what happened rather than an actual memory. The denial that soon set in caused Jim to doubt this experience.

Jim had never said anything about his father in the past that suggested he molested Jim. His father appeared to take little interest in his son. He was generous with criticism and stingy with compliments. He was similar to Jan's father in this respect, but Jan's father showed too much interest in her—the wrong kind of interest.

Though I helped Jim calm down a bit, he still left our session scared and confused. By our next session, he had mustered up his old defenses and felt distant from the feelings he'd had about the dream. Convinced that he had never been molested, Jim brushed off his earlier response as some kind of momentary delusion.

What does this dream tell us? For one thing, it's full of the symbolism that commonly appears in incest dreams. There is, for example, the action of the dreamer, bringing people to the horror scene, only to have the scene disappear altogether. Also evident is everyone else's scorn at his apparent hallucination. It's like the old detective movies where the hero discovers a body, only to have it disappear when witnesses are brought to the scene. The dream itself keeps the dreamer in a state of confusion. He does not want to believe that his father molested him, so he creates other people in the dream who can't see what he saw. Yet the frightening scene reappears in the dream, as if to confirm that it really happened. This could be a clue as to what took place in Jim's childhood. In most instances of incest, the assailant threatens to kill the victim if he tells. Sometimes the assailant threatens to harm someone dear to the victim, like a mother, a sibling, or a pet. The victim forgets that the incest took place out of denial and self-protection. It seems likely that this is what happened to Jim. In his dream he wanted others to validate that a terrible crime had been committed against him. He yearned for comfort and protection. Those impulses were stymied, however, by the likely threats of severe punishment if he ever told anyone, and in the dream he deals with his fear by making the scene disappear.

As noted earlier, broken bodies and detached limbs are frequent symbols in the dreams of incest victims. Jim's broken bodies are reminiscent of the doll with the missing limbs in Jan's dream. They symbolize the shattering of the self that occurs after an act of incest.

The location of the dream—the outskirts of town in the dreamer's childhood neighborhood—tells us something about when and where the incident occurred. It occurred, of course, in childhood ("childhood neighborhood"), perhaps in some remote place. It may have happened at a dump, but the dump is more likely a symbol for the way Jim felt when the incest happened (if it happened)—like garbage, dirty, discarded, and broken. This is exactly how the incest victim feels—discarded, thrown aside, of no value because of how inhumanly he or she has been treated. "Outskirts of town" could also represent what the dreamer pushes out of his awareness.

The most important thing about Jim's dream was that it brought the likely occurrence of incest to the surface. It gave him the opportunity to view and repair the damage that was done to him in childhood. Jim's deep anger and uncertainty about himself could have resulted from this destructive act against him. Having the actual memory of abuse, and, importantly, coming to terms with all the feelings surrounding it, offered him the chance of dramatically reducing the damage inflicted by those events.

If you have a dream of incest or other trauma, there are two things you should do: find a good therapist and join an incest victim group. Unfortunately, this phenomenon is proving more common than most people realize. Incest is no longer an unspoken secret, and there are bound to be incest support groups in your area.

Symbols for Your Dream Dictionary:

Bed: Place for sex.
Father: Godlike authority figure, protector.
Room: Womb, psyche.
Night: Darkness, secrets, the unconscious.
Index finger: Penis, aggressive gesture.
Mouth: Opening, expressiveness, female, vagina.
Gums: Internal organ.
Rim of mouth: Internal organ.
Left side: Shadow side, heart side.
Hand: Dexterity, creativity.
Wall: Barrier, defense, protection.
Underneath: Below the surface, not showing.
Boardwalk: Surface, what shows.
Bureau drawer: Hidden secrets.
Thigh: Sensual part of body.
Doll: Representation of child, child without life.
Missing limbs: Disintegration of self.
Card table: Exposing truths that have been concealed.
Street: Out in the open, dangerous.
Outskirts of town: On the edge, unacceptable, repressed.

Dump: Where leftovers, the used and the unwanted, are discarded.
Dismembered: Murdered, castrated.
Rats: Sexually repellent.

One valuable exercise for working with incest dreams (and other dreams as well) is the technique of continuing the dream while awake.

Exercise: Continue Your Dream While Awake

The idea is to continue the story of the dream to its conclusion. Be guided by any thoughts or memories or fantasies that come up. You can have a dream partner direct you, but the directions should come from you. If you're working with a dream partner, it's helpful to write down your directions on a sheet of paper, which your partner can then follow. Use the following as a guideline.

Start by getting into the same position you were in in the dream and close your eyes. Take deep breaths to help you relax. Then reenter the dream at any place you want. Tell your dream partner where you have reentered the dream and allow a dialogue to take place. Tell your dream partner exactly what you experience. Remember how entering the dump scene caused an emotional reaction in Jim? This occurred because the dreamer instinctively knows where to reenter the dream. The dream partner should let the dreamer choose what direction to go.

Your dream guide can ask you to describe your surroundings and what you are wearing in the dream. When characters enter the dream, have a dialogue with them. Your dream partner must allow himself to be guided by your answers. If, for example, you say you are standing in front of a dangerous person, your dream partner might ask you what you would like to say to this person. If you feel too frightened by the person, your dream partner should ask you who you would like to protect you and what you want that person to do. Both of you should utilize your imagination and creativity in the process.

It's also helpful to continue the dream where it left off. Discuss the dream with your dream partner and then have him ask you open-ended questions that guide you on the path you are already on. Neither your dream guide nor you should try to interpret anything. The object is to allow your imagination to take over and tell a story that really touches you inside. This is an excellent technique for uncovering hidden feelings and remembering buried memories.

NINE

An Art Museum
for the Blind

An art museum for the blind! Who could have dreamed up such a thing? A man who truly feels the need—Patrick Daniels, who is both blind and has AIDS. In response to these two challenges, Patrick undertook the enormous task of single-handedly bringing art to the blind in a new way. A year ago, when he had the following dream, the idea of an art museum for the blind had not even occurred to Patrick. The idea for this museum grew out of the dream itself. His has been a hero's journey ever since.

DREAM: *We're at a museum and my show is about to open in New York. The show is specifically designed for people who cannot see. The people in the dream are important members of New York society and intelligentsia. I recognize a couple who are in their fifties, like me. The woman has written a major book on a famous painter, and her husband is an editor at a prestigious publishing house. I am very pleased they are there, because I want them to like the exhibition I have assembled. I am excited that people I know are seeing it.*

We go down a hallway to the room where my exhi-

bition is supposed to be, but the room is empty. A guard says, "We took that exhibition down this afternoon." Feeling defeated, I stand in the void where my show should have been, not sure what to do next. Once again I have the all-too-familiar feeling of "What do you expect?" I try to brush it off with a sort of ironic comment, but I'm angry and embarrassed. The couple with me react with bemusement and condescension.

At the time of this dream, Patrick had been asked by the Commission on the Blind to write an article on art. The commission had chosen him because he was both a writer and a blind person. At the onset of his blindness in 1989, Patrick decided his education in art history was both absurd and useless, a total waste of time. Soon after the dream, however, Patrick realized that his dream gave him a powerful message: to bring art to the blind in a way that had never been done before. He has used every last ounce of energy to make his vision a reality.

When Patrick and I first looked at the dream, one meaning was immediately clear—the people who came to Patrick's show were sighted, and therefore could not experience what the blind experience. Thus for them, the exhibit did not exist. The dream also informed Patrick that he had not yet discovered a meaningful way to introduce blind people to the variety of insights and pleasure that art can provide. This realization led Patrick on a journey to discover for himself how the blind can appreciate art.

One year after this dream, Patrick and I met again. I wanted to find out if this dream had continued to have a major effect on him. He told me that the dream, along with the challenges of blindness and AIDS, had changed his life. The message in the dream gave Patrick something to live for, which he explained by detailing the events that followed the dream.

The dream, Patrick said, was an important stepping-stone to his new insights. It led him to discovering what blind people experience when they touch art, and what the blind can teach the sighted about art. "The blind," Patrick explained, "have a far greater appreciation and feeling for art than anybody suspects. They concentrate completely on what they feel. Through reading braille, they have developed a highly sensitive response to touch. They are accustomed to deriving meaning through their sense of touch. Many of the blind have had this faculty since childhood. I believe that the blind—if given the opportunity to learn—are going to teach the sighted a lot of things about art that they don't know.

"At a sculpture exhibition, a blind person can put his hand on a piece and learn more in five seconds than a sighted person can in fifteen minutes. With one gesture, the blind can comprehend many subtle aspects of the object that are invisible to even the most perceptive sighted observer. It's thrilling to have my hand follow the same motions that artists like Rodin, Matisse, and Picasso made when they created their works of art. The hands of those artists created those pieces by making certain gestures and forming certain shapes. My hand is right there where their hands were, tracing their path of creation. That is an incredible connection to a piece of art. Just looking at a work of art can't provide the same experience that touching does."

Patrick's dream transformed his life in another way, by enabling him to change a pattern that began in child-hood and continued up until the time of the dream. Patrick and I explored the feeling he experienced in his dream, since feelings are an immediate clue to a dream's meaning. I questioned him about his comment in the dream that "Once again I have the all-too-familiar feeling of 'What do you expect?' "

Patrick replied, "Until I had this dream, I always had a cynical attitude toward life. I guess I felt in the dream that I was in over my head and attempting to do something that I was not qualified to do. I felt exposed. It also seemed like I was in an uncooperative atmosphere and had no support. I was acting in a spirit of defiance. The dream does not explain how or why the exhibition was moved. It was almost divine intervention, or providence, or fate. When I said, 'What do you expect?' I meant it was just another example of the kind of disappointment and failure that always comes up for me. It's out of my control, like some fatalistic plan. I felt this was my fate or destiny, rather than something I created."

The seeds of Patrick's transformation are contained within the dream itself. The dream explains why it took Patrick fifty or more years to implement a project that could make such a difference in his own life and that of others. Until this realization, Patrick had felt a deep and persistent malaise, a feeling of "What's the use?" He saw himself as a lost soul, drifting through life with no purpose or direction. He didn't know who he was or why he was on earth. He knew he was intelligent and sensitive, but he didn't know how to use those qualities productively. He had no ambition or desire to pursue a career. There was no motivation for him to develop his abilities until he found out that he had AIDS five years ago. Suddenly he was face-to-face with the inescapable reality that his time on earth was severely limited. He thought to himself, If you're ever going to do anything with your life, you'd better do it now. Patrick's new-found sense of his own mortality lit a fire under him. At first he didn't know what course of action to take. But after having this dream, he took one step after another in the direction of the one thing that ultimately had the most meaning for him. Patrick claims that he's *never* been bored in the past five years. There was always something going on, something to think about, something to be involved in, something to do.

Why this happened can best be explained by looking at the dream again. The dream revealed that Patrick had a great need to influence others—it took place at a museum and it was *his* show that was about to open. The dream was set in one of the greatest art and cultural centers of the world, New York City, and the exhibit was designed for people who cannot see. This directly related to Patrick's mission, which was to bring art to the blind. However, the dream also uncovered an important psychological truth about Patrick: his feeling that people were unable to *see* what he was offering or who he was. The dream reflected both the practical matter of bringing art to the blind, as well as Patrick's perception about himself in relation to the rest of the world.

In his dream he arranged for two important people to view his show: an acclaimed writer and an important editor. They represented the idealized parental figures he had always wanted to acknowledge him. However, he also dreamed that his show was dismantled, indicating an anxiety that others would not appreciate what he was going to show them. The emotion that Patrick experienced in the dream was "the all-too-familiar feeling of 'What do you expect?'" That described Patrick's many disappointments in life and the way he relived them again and again. Although somewhere inside he was convinced that he had something to show, he was equally sure that no one would recognize it. We all tend to repeat early traumas until, hopefully, they are finally solved. Patrick's show falling apart illustrates yet another dream unfulfilled. The couple whom he wants to impress "react with bemusement and condescension."

This dream not only highlighted Patrick's lifelong feeling of failure, it also presented the solution to his problem, which is why it is a transformational dream. Patrick's desire for recognition had never been acknowledged. Ever since he was a small boy, his parents made it clear they had no time for him. His father was an arthritic alcoholic who was preoccupied with feeling powerless over these afflictions. His depression left him devoid of any positive energy to give Patrick. Patrick's mother, out of necessity, became the breadwinner of the family. She left Patrick and his father for months at a time. Patrick described her as a woman obsessed with making money, who ignored her own child while taking care of other people's children.

In the dream, Patrick yearned for recognition, but had nothing "to show" in order to gain that attention. Unaware of the parental neglect aspect of the dream, Patrick interpreted his dream to mean he was unprepared to have this exhibit. "When the exhibit disappeared in the dream," he said, "I realized it was because I hadn't done the requisite planning and thinking needed to get my ideas to the stage where they are now. The reason the gallery was empty might be because I hadn't done the work that I have done since then. This dream was a turning point in my life because it not only provided the idea for an exhibit, it also showed that something was missing, something that had to do with me."

The dream reflected Patrick's basic belief that something inside him was missing. This is a feeling children often get when their parents neglect them. Since children depend on their parents for their very survival, it feels safer to blame themselves rather than their parents for this lack of attention. The dream also gave Patrick the impetus to move forward in his life and provide for himself what was missing.

Dreams have many levels of meaning. Patrick responded to the dream in terms of his present reality, and it gave him the insight that he must take the steps needed to feel prepared to accomplish his goal. In his waking life, he implemented the actions necessary to resolve his lifelong trauma and fulfill his wish for recognition. The lack of acknowledgment from his parents had nothing to do with Patrick's actual potential. He had tremendous gifts that were overlooked. His parents induced in him a feeling of defeat, which was not based on fact. "My parents didn't want a creative child," Patrick stated. "They wanted an ordinary lump, a nine-to-five kind of person. I was terribly unhappy when I was young. The only way I survived was by finally running away from the torture, abuse, and alienation."

Because of a dream that explained emotionally and practically what he needed to know, Patrick at last took the courageous steps required to take hold of his life and realize his potential. Through his accomplishments he was able to give himself what his parents never gave him, and what every child so desperately needs—a feeling of self-worth.

Since becoming blind and developing AIDS, Patrick's life gained the type of direction and purpose that were previously lacking. His life had a purpose. "My life did not have meaning before," Patrick confided. "I think I'm now held together by a very strong sense of personal reality. I don't have that existential anxiety anymore. I no longer doubt myself. I may have AIDS, I may be blind, but psychologically I feel a thousand times better. It's wonderful to have a sense of self, a sense of purpose, a sense of value. That's what has happened to me since I got this so-called dreaded disease. I'm determined to stay alive as along as I possibly can. You have to have a reason to stay alive. If there's no purpose for your existence, it's hard to stay alive. I don't want to die because I've got to get my projects done."

When the Commission on the Blind originally asked Patrick to write an article on existing art programs, he believed that art was something he had written off, something he didn't want to even think about. Then, all of a sudden, he saw the possibility of appreciating art in a whole new way. "Since then, I feel that my passion and sense of urgency are invaluable. Most people who work on art programs aren't blind. Plus, the blind don't know anything about art and the sighted don't know anything about the blind. So I have this unique perspective, and this feeling and this passion, that is better than mere knowledge, because it doesn't just inform me, it motivates me as well. I *know* that art objects can be understood in a whole new way, in a new dimension. That's why I was so excited after the dream. What thrilled me was not so much the opportunity to gain personal prestige, but rather the possibility of bringing forward an exciting new insight into art objects.

"In the meantime, I have supplied the missing elements in the dream. I have done the kind of work and thinking that I hadn't done at the time of the dream. I don't think if I had a similar dream today, the gallery would be empty. I *know* what that exhibit would be. When I imagine a museum for the blind, I know what objects would be in it and why. I understand what those objects mean and how their meaning can be conveyed to the blind. One of my proposals to MOMA (The Museum of Modern Art) illustrates how to convey the whole progression of modern design through chairs, beginning in 1894 with Art Nouveau and going to the most streamlined and abstract new designs today. Let the blind sit in those chairs. Let the object hold them. Let them feel it and understand how it's made. Then, while someone is sitting in a chair, I could give him an art object that reinforces the design of the chair. That way he's holding the object and the chair is holding him, and he is intimately connected to the idea of that particular design. If you did that ten times, boy, the blind would know something at the end of that visit that they didn't know at the beginning.

"People get upset when you talk about three dimensions because they have a 'don't touch' attitude toward art. That's why I think a museum for the blind is the ultimate answer. It will deal exclusively with the way that art objects and the blind can interact.

"The dream was the beginning of all this. It was the subconscious catalyst for all this activity."

On August 10, 1994, Governor Mario Cuomo designated Patrick to be the New York State ADA (Americans with Disabilities Act of 1982) Advocate specializing in blindness issues. This enabled him to implement his ideas.

Symbols for Your Dream Dictionary:

Museum: A place where society's achievements are stored and displayed. Outer recognition of inner worth.

Society: Highest form of public opinion.

Couple: Parents.

Painter: Someone who expresses the unconscious visually.

Editor: Censor.

Publishing house: Producer of written and visual creations that are acceptable for the public.
Hallway: Passageway to the unconscious.
Exhibition: Intimate self-revelation.
Guard: Barrier.

Exercise: Listen to Music to Mirror and Cultivate Your Feelings

We need to practice delving deeper into our feelings as a way to access the messages of our dreams. Whereas working with dreams leads to the feelings contained within them, sensitivity to feelings allows us to be more in touch with our feelings as we work with our dreams. Learning to let our feelings flow with music is excellent practice for this. Stopping and controlling feelings, as many of us have learned to do, is a deterrent to gaining your dream's message. Patrick was fortunate that no one interfered with his feelings as a child. Since neither of his parents mirrored his feelings, he looked elsewhere for reflection and expression of them. The parental neglect he experienced ironically gave him a lot of freedom. Through music he gained access to the wide range of emotional nuances that have enriched his life. When you want to be more in touch with both the feelings in your life *and* in your dreams, simply turn on your stereo or radio and let yourself be completely carried away by the music. If you notice a tendency to stop a feeling, discover where you are holding it in your body, breathe into it, and let the tension go.

TEN

The Screaming Baby

The patient, whom I will call Angela, was tormented all her life by obsessive thoughts of animals being tortured. During our sessions, she reported every horrible accident she saw, down to the most minute, bloody detail. She replayed these incidents over and over in her mind, to the point where they kept her up all night. On those infrequent occasions that she briefly dozed off, she dreamed about starving, abandoned animals and invariably woke up to images of dead and injured ones. She knew something was wrong, since her preoccupation with animals outweighed her concern for humans. She saw a dog get hit by a car one day, then watched her neighbor rush toward the dog to save it. Knowing the dog was being attended to, she hurried away from the scene, unable to bear the sight of the dog writhing on the ground. Despite her best efforts, the picture of the wounded dog remained firmly fixed in her mind. The next day, she asked the neighbor about the dog and was relieved to hear the veterinarian had saved the dog's life. In contrast, Angela never inquired about the neighbor's wife, who was dying of cancer at the time. She felt guilty about her lack of interest.

Angela's husband derided her for leaving the room whenever an animal was injured or mistreated on TV. Though a member of several animal rights organizations, Angela dumped their flyers and magazines into the trash unopened. She couldn't risk seeing pictures or headlines of animal atrocities.

Angela entered therapy because her life seemed empty and she felt betrayed by family and friends. Not surprisingly, she also complained about feeling depressed. Although her obsession with animals was not what brought her to therapy, it became a dominant theme as the therapy progressed.

We had worked on her problem for several years, and the therapy had improved certain aspects of her life. She was more successful in her career as a financial analyst, her relationship with her husband was better, and she was more outgoing with other people. But her despair, feelings of abandonment, and obsession with hurt animals remained the same. Only recently had she begun to feel some of the sadness and anger that was at the root of her depression, and address it during our sessions. While suffering a particularly difficult bout of depression, she had this dream:

DREAM: *It is nighttime. I hear a kitten wailing. I run to look for it, and find a starving, decrepit kitten. I pick it up, comfort it, and put it in a cloth satchel that hangs from my shoulder. I am relieved that I have found the hungry kitten, and vow to take care of it. But after a few moments, the wailing resumes, and it's not coming from the kitten. It turns into nonstop, inconsolable screaming. I rush to the place where the screaming is coming from. I end up under a building structure—it's very dark. Then I step out onto a well-lit plaza. It looks like San Marco Square in Venice, Italy. There, on the cold stone pavement, is a fat, red-cheeked infant in swaddling clothes. It's all alone, screaming at the top of its lungs. I run for*

*help, and wake up thinking, Why didn't I go directly
to the baby? Why did I run for help? Next time, I'll
pick up the baby and comfort it.*

Angela was encouraged by this dream, because she
understood one of its messages. Throughout her adulthood she had had recurrent dreams of kittens crying and
had always tried to rescue them. This dream showed her
that the kittens were only a disguise—she projected her
feelings of abandonment and pain onto them. This
dream pointed out that the source of her pain was her
own abandoned baby self.

Angela had never experienced this pain as her own.
She always attached the pain to something outside herself, something external. Her anguish over the pain of
injured animals was really an expression of her own terror. Since the baby was all alone, the dream suggested
that this pain had been inflicted by neglectful adults.
The baby in the dream was healthy and well fed, but no
one was caring for it. The animals in her dreams, on the
other hand, were starving, which symbolized Angela's
emotional starvation. Furthermore, Angela goes from
darkness to light in the dream, suggesting that she was
no longer in the dark about the truth. The dream was a
breakthrough, evidence that she was strong enough now
to go to the real source of her pain. As previously
noted, dreams do not disclose anything we are not ready
to face. Angela no longer had the unconscious need to
hide her own suffering behind the suffering of helpless
animals.

This dream illustrates two characteristics of dreams.
One is the transformation of one symbol into another
(here, the kitten turns into the infant). The other is the
introduction of a new element (the baby) into a recurrent dream. The changing of one symbol into another

during a dream is the dream's way of giving up one disguise for a disguise that is truer to the dreamer's real feelings. The dream is in sync with the psyche. Thanks to her previous dreamwork and her own intuition, Angela knew the baby represented herself. Once Angela can feel all the feelings of the dream infant in her waking life, she will no longer have the need to dream about abandoned kittens or babies. A symbol becomes obsolete once we become conscious of its meaning.

The introduction of a new element into a recurrent dream is a cause for celebration. It means that part of the dreamer's defensive structure has weakened, permitting something new to come forward. It's like the proverbial peeling of the onion, where each layer reveals something new. Working through our defenses is like cleaning the lenses of eyeglasses—it gives a clearer picture of who we truly are. We are able to see parts of ourselves, and parts of the world, that were invisible to us before. That discovery is exciting and gives us hope. The unconscious cooperates by revealing its treasures when, and only when, we are ready. For that reason, dreams are trustworthy friends—they do not push or prod us, or throw us into tailspins by upsetting our balance. Instead, they move along with us at a pace we can tolerate.

Not only did this dream give Angela insight, but it also determined the direction of our work together. The therapy that followed this dream integrated her insight into her psyche and led to remarkable changes in her.

Before her breakthrough dream, Angela was unable to consistently trust the important people in her life. She had been married for three years, yet still needed constant reassurance from her husband that he cared for her. In fact, her trust wavered toward everyone who was important to her. She frequently reported that her husband had betrayed or disappointed her. "I don't need to analyze why I dislike him so much today," she often said. "It's partly because I was beginning to trust him, and once again he revealed that he had very little energy for me. I can't stand seeing him smile, pleased at the idea that he has the power to hurt my feelings. I hate his superiority, his arrogance, his feeling so pleased with himself. I'm sorry I gave him credit for anything, because it just feeds his ego. For a split second I felt a tinge of hurt, because his interest in his own ego is far greater than his interest in me. Is this what 'male' means to me?"

The people who seemed to care the most, Angela said, were also the ones most capable of deeply hurting her. Once she began to trust them, she fell prey to her childhood vulnerabilities and dependencies. The fact that she intellectually understood that it was her past hurts that caused her to overreact changed nothing, and only gave her a *reason* for her feelings. Her sister forgot a lunch date with her, and Angela said: "I'm tired of focusing on the unpleasant—such as the depression following my sister's no-show. For my own self-esteem, and perhaps to avoid future depressions, I should drop her for good. It sounds mean, but think of the kind of trial by fire she put me through. If she doesn't forget to meet me, she's late. Why do I put up with her? Because she's my sister? She takes me for granted and abuses me—not with words, but with behavior. Oh, the choice words I'd like to use on her!"

Angela's perception that others abused her turned her anger into vindictiveness. That reaction, combined with her constant doubt of their love, made her a difficult person to be around at times.

The feelings of abandonment often came out as fear. During therapy, I asked her what was behind that fear.

And she replied, "I know what it is even without letting the feeling come up—my own lack of self-worth. But if that is true, why don't I let myself feel *that* rather than the terror?" Terror and anxiety, as awful as they can be, are often all the ego can tolerate. The pain of really believing she was worth nothing was more than Angela could bear. It is no wonder children defend themselves from these feelings by convincing themselves they are loved when they are not. The truth could destroy their motivation for living.

As Angela and I worked together to free her real feelings, she got in touch with her original abandonment, the one that led to her belief that she was not worth much. She often complained that she was tired of waking up every morning afraid. "I'd like to go to sleep just one night," she said, "and wake up without fear—fear that I've been rejected, fear that no one will be there for me."

One month before her big dream, Angela remembered her helplessness, how she held on to her mother for survival and panicked when her mother left her at school. It made her think of a younger cousin, who became dependent on Angela as a child. Now an adult, her cousin emotionally blackmailed Angela for money. Her cousin expressed such feelings of despair and helplessness that Angela thought of her as one of the abandoned kittens of her dreams. As much as she wanted to, there was no way Angela could refuse her. Angela now understood why she never ended this relationship—she imagined that her cousin's feelings toward her were the same as Angela's toward her mother. "I'm enraged with her like mother was with me. Mother's feeling was, 'Get off my back.'"

I explained to Angela that what her cousin, now an adult, did to her, and what Angela, as a child, did to her mother were two different things. Although I tried to introduce a little reality into the situation, I knew it might not help. The imprints of childhood are deep and difficult to change. Angela believed her mother saw her as a leech, someone who was interfering with her freedom. She thought her mother wanted to get away from her. But thankfully, that insight did make a difference, because Angela now understood that was no way for a mother to treat a helpless child. This realization made her feel her anger, which was what she needed to do to free herself. She was finally able to verbalize that her mother was a mean mother, a betrayer who walked out on her. It was clear that her mother didn't care about her, and just wanted to get away from her. But then Angela concluded, "I must not be any good if she wanted to leave me so much." (Angela's mother was a woman who felt too helpless and guilty to get her own needs met. She acted out her ambivalence, and although it might not have been her intention, her conflict produced deep feelings of rejection in Angela.)

When Angela's husband, a photographer, went away on a shoot she reacted as if he had gone away forever. This is how an infant feels when its mother leaves it alone, and was another indication that Angela had not worked through her early feelings. When her husband was away, she truly believed that there was no living presence in her life to love, care, and worry about her. There was no deep bond, nobody who knew of her deepest concerns. "What about me?" I would ask. She replied, "Oh, you're just my therapist." She fluctuated between believing I was really there for her to feeling I didn't care. Just like her mother.

Although Angela admitted she did have some moments of pleasure, she also thought there was no underlying reason for her life if love is the main reason for living. She felt that her existence did not mean much to anyone. Rationally she understood that her husband had to go away for work. But emotionally she believed he had abandoned her because he did not love her. She then withdrew and felt hopeless. About three weeks before her dream, she described the pain she was feeling as "a stifled cry, even a scream. Perhaps a primal scream having to do with feeling that I'm no one." As Angela became more aware of her feelings, her unconscious reorganized and elaborated upon this information—and got ready to present her with some truths she would now be able to take in. This is a perfect example of how waking life and dreaming life are inextricably entwined.

The dream awakened Angela to her true inner suffering. She was an abandoned baby who no one picked up when she screamed. Her screen memory—a memory of a real event that's used as a cover for another, more important, similar real event that is too traumatic to remember—of her mother not picking her up at school was as much as she had been able to remember. I started working with Angela on this dream by asking her to lie down on the floor mat and become the baby. Reluctantly she agreed to cooperate. When I asked her to scream like the dream baby, she became angry and resistant. How could she do that? she asked. She wasn't feeling it now. "Imitate the scream," I suggested. She did, and soon the imitation became real. A stream of memories came forth about how she and her mother interacted when she was an infant. This was a powerful session, and during the next two weeks important insights followed as a result.

During that session she reexperienced how physically remote her mother was. She desperately wanted her mother to pick her up, hold her, and tell her that she loved her. But her mother was preoccupied with her own concerns and was perhaps uneasy about handling a baby. There were times when the bond between them was "exquisite, beautiful," Angela said. Angela recalled the feelings, not the actual memories. But they were so real that she knew they must have occurred. As a child, Angela kept trying to recapture that state of bliss with her mother by asking over and over for reassurance. This irritated her mother, which guaranteed that Angela would never get what she wanted. She never felt sure of her mother's love, always thinking she had to win it by being a good girl. She repetitively asked her mother, "Am I a good girl?" In her present life, Angela played out the same scenario with her husband and the other people who were close to her. They, too, became irritated with her excessive demands.

Sometimes her mother loved her, but not often enough. Plus, her mother never told her she loved her and often yelled at Angela in a way that made Angela feel she hated her. Parents can't be expected to be saints—and are certainly entitled to get impatient with their children. But when they don't let their children know they still love them even though they are impatient or angry, they implant in their children feelings of worthlessness and rejection. When her mother withdrew, Angela experienced the withdrawal as Paradise Lost. Angela sobbed plentiful tears as she realized this old pain.

Many changes took place in Angela after her dream. Her preoccupation with hurt, abandoned animals disappeared. She still cared about what happened to them, but she didn't obsess about them as she had before. Overcoming this fear enabled her to accompany her husband, a wildlife photographer, on some of his assignments. Not only did Angela step out into the world more, she also avoided the painful separations from her husband. Additionally, she no longer perceived herself as unlovable, and, therefore, didn't constantly ask for reassurance. Imprints from childhood are never totally erased, but they can be reduced significantly so that the person can live a much happier, more fulfilled life. Angela continued to work out these early imprints and was sometimes able to stop herself when she began reacting with rejection or despair to an outside event. She reminded herself that these feelings were from the past and were not caused by what was happening at that moment.

Another significant change was that she was less angry with her husband. Her previous doubt of his love had led to many arguments between them. At that time, she felt neglected by everyone. Those bad feelings have greatly diminished because Angela now knows she wasn't abandoned by her mother because she was no good, but rather because her mother was an inadequate mother.

Once she heard the screaming baby inside *her,* Angela realized that her cousin's begging and desperation was unbearable because of her own feelings, not her cousin's. She no longer reacted as strongly to her cousin's "screaming baby" and recognized that she was being manipulated for money. It became easier to say no. This also significantly reduced her arguments with her husband, since he was greatly put out by the cousin's requests and reprimanded Angela for giving in to her.

By continuing to feel the roots of her pain, Angela was able to heal.

Symbols for Your Dream Dictionary:
Nighttime: The unconscious, something hidden.
Kitten: Symbol of vulnerable child.

Satchel: Womb.
Darkness: The unconscious.
Well-lit Area: The conscious mind, enlightened.
Venice: City of warmth and fun.
Plaza: Space for expansion, possibilities, the center of
   things.
Stone: Cold, inhuman.

Exercise: Draw While You Tell Your Dream

Angela's dream tapped into the deep feelings that subsequently brought about transformation. In a follow-up
session, she doodled as she talked to me about the
dream. Quite spontaneously she drew the baby in her
dream. This drawing brought out even more meanings.
Angela looked at her drawing of the fat, healthy baby
and realized that her mother had never neglected her material comforts as a child, only her emotional needs. The
drawing helped her to process more feelings. Once
again, she felt her familiar frazzled, tentative sense of
self-worth—and her fear of being sent into the raw terror
of abandonment and extinction. She knew she could easily be torn asunder, damaged through hurt, and made to
feel worthless, like someone who had been discarded, an
outsider and a misfit. She recognized that she didn't have
enough human companionship, just as there hadn't been
enough of her mother's love. She sensed the indifference
of the world, and suffered profound grief. She experienced all the feelings that resulted from an accurate picture of her relationship with her mother. The more she
felt it at its source, the less it would reappear in her
present-day life.

Drawing is an excellent way for you to get into your
feelings, too. Both Freud and Jung realized that dreams
are pictures of feelings and sensations and that drawing
is a direct route to the unconscious. These two great

men each said that drawings can reveal aspects of a dream image that words alone cannot. In addition, the drawing can elicit new and unexpected associations.

So if you wish to get to the deeper meanings of your dream, spontaneously draw the most intriguing symbol of your dream while telling the dream to a trusted friend or therapist. Spontaneous drawing is similar to doodling.

Spontaneous, rather than descriptive, drawing is nondirective and stems from your unconscious. (The phrase "spontaneous drawing" is derived from the work of art therapist Margaret Naumberg.) When I say it is synonymous with doodling, I mean that you produce images from your unconscious while you are speaking, thinking or not thinking, or remaining silent. Do not consider what you are doing to be art, and you will neither be self-conscious nor judgmental about these expressions. During spontaneous drawing, you needn't shift your attention away from any thoughts you might have.

In addition, doodling can be a form of relaxation and a distraction from conscious thought. It is often a better mirror of what is going on inside you than the words you may be expressing. By doing this exercise you may rediscover the cliché that "One picture is worth a thousand words." It is a very effective technique, so try it with any of your dreams.

ELEVEN

Crashing Through
the Waves

DREAM: *I'm standing waist deep in the ocean. In the distance I see huge black tidal waves coming toward me. They grow in size as they approach me. I realize I will be swallowed up and destroyed by them. I'm gripped by terror as I envision my life disappearing. Then I decide it's sink or swim. I make up my mind to meet the waves head-on. A wave swells toward me, huge and powerful. I plunge through it and come out the other side. I survive. I am triumphant.*

The dreamer, whom I shall call Claire, felt ecstatic after this dream, and it was followed by a week full of successes. This was no mere coincidence, because as Claire's attitudes began to change, so did her life. The dream showed her that if she didn't fight back, she would be swallowed up. Yet if she did fight back, she might feel as if she were dying. (Whenever we dramatically change our lives by replacing a past pattern of behavior with a new one, we often feel as if we're dying.) During the dream, Claire had to make a choice: either run from the waves or face them. Her choice of fighting back came from her subconscious. Her determination to survive was so powerful that choosing to confront the waves in her dream led to significant changes in her waking life. It took great bravery to face that overpowering tidal wave, and she had done it.

A dream like Claire's suggests great inner turmoil. What was it that Claire had to fight against? These were her words when she first came to therapy:

I didn't want to have to do this, to come to therapy. My family already thinks I'm a loser. Stan, my husband, is beginning to feel that way, too. He told me to get help. I feel if I don't, he'll leave me. He hates that I'm overweight. I try very hard to lose weight. I diet, I exercise. Then I ruin it all. I let everything go to pieces—the house, the kids. I escape from everything by reading trash novels and bingeing on sweets.

I try to hide from my husband that I'm bingeing. I feel like a closet drinker. I'm terrified that he'll leave me. I don't know what I'll do if that happens.

I don't know why I hate myself so. I'm not successful at anything I do. My husband wants me to get a part-time job. He makes a good living, but he's insecure about money. He thinks the money is going to stop coming in, even though he has a successful veterinary practice. We have two kids. When the youngest child was ten years old, my husband told me to get a part-time job and help out financially.

The most frustrating part is that I know I'm a creative person, but I can't seem to tap into it. I don't even have a clue about which direction to pursue. My husband says, 'Get a job, any job.' I listen to him and I take jobs that are beneath my abilities, and then get fired from them anyway.

In a way my husband's just like my parents. They always thought I'd fail at anything I did. Their expectations for me were nil. Before I got married, they also told me to take any old job. They wanted me off their hands, so they wouldn't have to worry about me. The bottom line is they don't want to deal with me. When I got pregnant as a teenager my mother treated me like I was a whore. She said I was a disgrace to the family. Ironically, she worked in a pregnancy crisis center at the time.

I didn't want my parents to help me out with my pregnancy. I admitted myself to a clinic for unwed mothers and assured my parents I'd be all right. I asked them to take a vacation while I had the baby. It was very hard for me, but it was better than meeting my mother's disapproving eyes and feeling the shame. I didn't want to listen to their constant reminders that I had disappointed them. How long could I keep hearing, 'You've gone against every family value we ever taught you. You don't even deserve to be in this family,' before I cracked up? I told my mother that I'd have the baby alone and that she didn't have to worry about me, I'd be all right. At least I could try to please them in one way, by handling this without them. They had taught me to be self-sufficient and completely independent, capable of doing everything on my own, without help. I learned to figure things out for myself and never asked them for anything. Even though I felt scared and alone, I assured them that their assistance was unnecessary. I was thirteen years old at the time. They said okay.

I learned to hate my body, to hate what was inside it. . . . I probably would have never gotten pregnant again if Stan hadn't insisted on having kids. I sometimes wonder why he made such a fuss about it. He hardly ever talks to them. He expects me to discipline them and deal with all their problems by myself.

Stan is disappointed in me, and I sense my kids are, too. They wonder why I can't get it together. When I'm depressed, all I do is read and binge on sweets. . . . And I'm depressed a lot.

Claire hid her true feelings from everyone and maintained a cheerful, helpful facade. Her friends would have been shocked to know that she had been severely depressed all her life, and especially now. Terror lurked behind her friendly exterior. What if she never found her niche in life? What if her husband left her? What if she was failing her children? These anxieties were invisible to others, for Claire dealt with them silently and stoically for years, never burdening anyone else with them.

When Claire entered therapy, she didn't understand why she felt that she had no self. She was bitterly disappointed in herself. She didn't know what she wanted to do in life. Since she always blamed herself for everything, she was surprised to learn during the course of the therapy that, in fact, everything wrong wasn't her fault. For one thing, her husband was an extremely difficult man. She saw that he was tyrannical, critical, distant, and demanding—very much like her mother. He laid down the law and refused to accept an opposing point of view. Plus, he insisted everything be done according to his strict standards. Everyday family dinners were conducted with the utmost dignity and formality. Their two children always had to be perfectly mannered and dressed. They were not to make noise in his presence or disturb him. It was Claire's habit to put his needs and everybody else's before her own. She managed to keep the house and the children immaculate whenever she could, but then she'd frequently become overwhelmed with depression. She'd pour herself into trashy novels and binge on chocolate, all to escape her feelings of frustration and failure. The bingeing not only added to her weight but to her husband's scorn.

As we continued to work together, her dissatisfactions—and their underlying causes—became more apparent. She recognized that her tendency to put the needs of others before her own had its origin in childhood. Her parents taught her to fend for herself at an early age and never to ask for help. Not only did they ignore her needs, they also made demands on her that were impossible for any child to meet. Her parents bickered frequently between themselves, and Claire soon learned that asking for help not only angered them but burdened them as well. This inhibition left her feeling helpless and stupid when she didn't know how to do things.

Claire believed the reason her mother was so intolerant of weakness was because her mother was crippled from childhood by infantile paralysis. She learned to survive through sheer willpower and controlled the world from her wheelchair. Claire's mother believed in the puritanical work ethic, and gave Claire responsibilities that were way beyond her capacities. Despite her background, my patient was a dreamer and had a secret life of her own. It was full of poetry, a place where her true self resided and could not be destroyed. This was Claire's strength.

When Claire was twelve, her father asked her to bring five hundred dollars to a neighbor for a down payment on a sailboat. On her way, Claire stopped off to buy ice cream. Some young delinquents noticed the money, threw her to the ground, beat her up, and took the five hundred dollars. She ran home, crying and ashamed, but covered up her tears when she got there. Her mother blamed her for what had happened and insisted she earn back the money. Her parents seemed to forget she was only a child. The neighbor, who was more lenient, said she could pay off the debt by doing errands and work around his house after school.

This was only one of many experiences that left Claire feeling abandoned and alone. She was fearful of making mistakes because she felt that no one would bail her out or even support her.

Claire's husband was not much better than her mother. He nagged her when things were not the way he wanted. He treated her more like a servant or a child than an equal. Her husband firmly believed that men deserved to be catered to by women. When Claire came into therapy, she accepted that this was the way things were. She blamed herself for not living up to his standards—and felt she got the treatment she deserved. But her resentment grew as she realized how stifling he was. As she began to push back at her husband and refuse to let him discourage her, she also became aware that she was symbolically working out her relationship with her mother. Her husband, in turn, began to yield a little bit to her needs and made an effort to listen to her.

Her creativity also began to blossom as she recalled times in childhood when she drew and painted—an activity that her mother dismissed. Claire had painted when she was alone, which was most of the time. One day her mother discovered what she was doing, and Claire stopped. She feared her mother's harsh criticism and her complaints that Claire was not doing enough around the house. The love of art became her secret, which she shared with no one. After a while, she forgot about it.

As Claire began to paint again, she started fighting back even more when her husband was domineering. She discovered she was beginning to like herself more.

Her self-expression seemed to go hand in hand with her anger toward her mother. Instead of feeling she, Claire, was flawed, she realized her mother was the one who didn't measure up. She stopped trying to please her mother, which never worked anyway, and began to value herself more. Claire still wanted to express her creativity in a tangible, practical way, but she didn't know how. She desperately wanted to paint, but also yearned for something that would connect her to the outside world.

If her family had ever discovered that she was painting, they would have considered it sheer self-indulgence, an enormous waste of time. On the few occasions that her family praised her, it was only for doing things she hated. Her husband merely humored her in her painting. It never occurred to him that she might have talent. It was in this unsupportive atmosphere that her first tidal-wave dream was born. This dream occurred several months before the turning-point dream at the beginning of this chapter. People frequently have recurrent dreams about the dysfunctional areas in their lives. This was Claire's preliminary tidal-wave dream:

DREAM: *I'm at the beach. Someone says the waves are not high. I go into the water. In the distance I see the highest wave I've ever seen, as tall as a building. Midway between this wave and the shore is a very low wave. In the foreground is another wave, which is not quite as high as the one in the distance. I scurry out of the water. The sight is magnificent— deep blue water with sparkling white waves. But there are so many people on the beach I feel there is no room for me. I get into the backseat of a car and watch the ocean from there.*

When Claire associated to this dream, she thought that being in the backseat of the car meant being separated and protected from the primal world. The dream indicated her awareness of her deep feelings (the tidal waves) and her feelings of danger. At this stage she lacked the confidence to meet them head-on. She retreated, as usual, to the backseat—a passive position.

When Claire had her turning-point dream, it was not the dream per se but the action Claire took in the dream—charging into the waves—that changed her life. Unlike Mark's dream (Chapter One: "The Token Dispenser"), Claire's dream did not require exploration of the symbols and metaphors for transformation to occur. The full meaning of the dream evolved during the course of therapy, and helped her solidify her experience.

Claire discovered immediate results from her transformational dream. The first was in the sexual sphere. Her husband was uninterested in sex and rarely wanted to make love. After the dream, instead of waiting for her husband to initiate sex, she seduced him. They had real intimacy for the first time since they were married. The sex, she said, was great.

A second result was that she demanded her husband give her space in the apartment to paint. He had appropriated the one unused bedroom in their spacious apartment for his own purposes, without asking her. It was a room for his junk, his papers, and the dogs he occasionally brought home from the clinic. Although he didn't surrender this room, she felt gratified that she had at least stated her wishes strongly.

Third, she wrote her mother a scathing letter in which she accused her of taking control of her (Claire's) life without ever acknowledging her needs. She spared nothing, and was pleased with her effort. She gave her mother a taste of her own medicine, hoping her mother would feel the vulnerability she had felt as a child. The letter was the first time she asserted herself with her martinet of a mother. The very act of writing it, and then sending it, empowered Claire.

In addition, Claire insisted her husband hang some of her paintings in his clinic's waiting room. One of his clients loved her work and bought a painting. This acknowledgment gave her the confidence she needed to plunge further into her work, instead of retreating into self-doubt. Expressing herself creatively was more rewarding because she finally believed in herself.

Lastly, Claire made up her mind once and for all to stop trying to make everyone comfortable. She decided to disagree with people if she felt like it, even if they withdrew their support.

Claire benefited from the dream without knowing its full meaning, because her dream action carried over into life. Once we master a feeling or situation in our dreams, we can do the same thing in our waking lives, sometimes without even thinking about it. The die has been cast. A dream like Claire's, which is both vivid and dramatic, is bound to have a powerful effect.

However, discovering the exact meaning of her dream also greatly benefited Claire. It helped her understand herself better—and also served to remind her, during those times when her old patterns reappeared, what those patterns veiled and what actions she could take to rectify the situation.

The immediate effects of the dream occurred the week following the dream. The other changes—and they were significant—happened within two or three months after the dream. These later changes were related to her understanding her dream and its message.

Let us go into the dream now and see what it means.

There is, first of all, the obvious message of the dream—that Claire must confront the obstacles, over-whelming though they may be, that threaten to destroy her. However, these obstacles were not specified by the dream. What were they?

To understand this, let us look at the most prominent symbol in Claire's dream—the tidal waves. Tidal waves in a dream usually represent feelings of being over-whelmed. So if you dream of tidal waves, ask yourself what in your present life feels as if it is too much to handle. People can be overwhelmed by any number of phenomena—illness, death, financial insecurity, marital problems, and troubled children, for example—and the feelings that accompany them. Tidal waves can also represent repressed feelings, feelings that have been contained until now, rising to the surface. Because they have been repressed, they now seem huge and out of control. Contained feelings build up inside like a pres-sure cooker until the person feels ready to explode. When feelings are expressed naturally, as they arise, the pressure does not build and the release of the feelings is comfortable.

Another important symbol in Claire's dream was the color black. Colors are important clues to the dream's meaning. Black was a dead giveaway in this case, be-cause the patient had spent her whole life fighting depression—and the color black is often associated with depression. However, black can be connected with other phenomena, too, such as death, the shadow, evil. Addi-tional meanings for black depend on the personal asso-ciations of the dreamer. The meanings of the symbols in a dream become more exact the more we learn about the individual dreamer. The meaning of Claire's dream gained clarity as the therapy proceeded.

Another clue to the dream's meaning was the patient's position in the water. She was not at the edge of the ocean, which would have suggested a person coming to a major crossroads and having to decide whether or not to take the plunge. Claire was waist-high in water. This indicates that she was already partially immersed and involved in the situation or feelings that evoked this dream.

In the dream Claire crashes through an enormous black wave, which is indicative of her willingness to confront her fears, rather than run away from them as she had in the past. By mustering up her bravery, she reached a turning point. Instead of giving up and staying in her rut, she was now willing to feel her frustrations and battle them out like a brave soldier. Her eyes filled with tears of self-appreciation when she realized this.

What brought her to this place? Was it the recognition that she could not go on living as before? Was she coming to terms with the painful fact that her life was going by and if she wanted a fulfilled life she had to make it happen now? Was she finally fed up with repeating the same defeating patterns year after year? Was she gaining confidence from the self-expression that had already taken place? Was she finally in a position where she experienced her life as something of value, something she could actively take hold of, and not something she had to passively endure? Her dream action was one of superlative courage. She was ready to fight for her life, even if she died in the process.

Unless you have a lucid dream (a dream in which you know you are dreaming), you are not aware that you are dreaming. Thus, there is no difference in your psyche between combatting a tidal wave in waking reality or in dream reality. Claire survived; she came out on the other side. Another person having a dream of oncoming tidal waves might have dreamed a different outcome—such as waking up with a start at the moment the waves crashed down. People often awaken from dreams at a moment of intense fear. Or another dreamer might have dreamed of being thrown to the ground by the wave, gasping for air, and drowning. Someone else might have seen the tidal waves approaching and run away.

Claire's dream indicated that she was getting much stronger. She was no longer content to bury her bad feelings and simply survive. She was willing to fight the overwhelming forces. The waves revealed to her the magnitude and force of what she was up against. Although she might not have been aware of just how great her battle was, the dreams made obvious—as dreams do—the odds she was not conscious of.

As Claire gained more clarity about her pattern of putting everyone else's needs before her own, she resented the relatives who took advantage of her. Before, she had not minded the impositions. She was known, after an exhausting day of meeting her own family's needs, to good-naturedly prepare flower arrangements for other people's dinner parties. Friends would ask her advice on their wardrobes, their home furnishings, and how to dress their kids. They recognized her artistic gifts and took her generosity for granted. Previously, she never thought of these abilities as talents. In fact, she took them for granted herself. But once she saw that they had value, she resented giving them away for nothing. This resentment was one of her initial steps toward liberation.

Some weeks after her dream, her feelings of depression returned. Claire said she didn't know what her depression was about, but she was determined, for the first time, to fight the depression (via her dream). What was it she had fought in her dream? Waves. It seemed that the waves, especially the black ones, did, in fact, stand for depression. Claire recognized that one of her biggest enemies was her depression. This time she did not allow herself to sink back into reading trash novels and bingeing on chocolate. She knew she had to fight, and she did it by painting and by continuing to fight with her husband for space in which to work. She argued with him about the extra room that was now a storehouse for his junk. She needed her own space, "a room of her own," as the novelist Virginia Woolf wrote about so movingly in 1929.

But the waves also represented something else. Dreams can have many levels of meaning, and one symbol can stand for many things. Her depression reappeared when a college friend stayed in her apartment. Claire's husband had to go out of town for his annual veterinarians' conference. This friend, who lived abroad, came to New York and asked Claire to put her up for a day or two. Claire said yes. But as it turned out, the friend stayed three nights, didn't volunteer to help out, and didn't leave Claire alone for a second. With her husband away, this would have been an ideal time for Claire to paint. She told the friend right from the start that she wanted to paint one afternoon, hoping the friend would take the hint and leave the apartment. But all she did was hang around and talk to her while she was painting. The friend, remembering the old Claire, expected her to wait on her hand and foot. Claire tactfully tried to learn when the friend would be leaving. Her inner voice, however, was screaming, When the f—— is she going to get out of here? Apparently "never" was the answer, since the friend made no mention of leaving. Claire confronted her. The friend was angry and felt betrayed. But Claire stood her ground and told the friend she must leave the next morning. Interestingly, the depression left immediately. Before the confrontation, Claire had binged on sweets. When she asserted herself, her desire to eat sweets immediately disappeared. In the past she would have stuffed all her feelings down with food. Claire realized that overeating was her unsuccessful way of coping with unpleasant feelings.

So the waves not only represented depression but anger. The two frequently go hand in hand. Depression is often unexpressed anger that turns against the self because it has nowhere else to go.

As Claire spoke about the absence of her need to eat compulsively, she remembered an old pattern from childhood. She would secretly sneak cookies from the dining room table to her room at night and then savor them slowly in bed. This memory was followed by others, of screaming and crying for her mother to come and take care of her. But her mother never came. These repressed memories reflected Claire's early oral needs and were the key to understanding the underlying cause of her lifelong depression. Claire's mother neglected Claire's needs as a small child, which led to rage on Claire's part. The rage resulted in depression because it was never expressed. Claire allowed herself to feel the pain of that early deprivation; it was the path to conquering the depression and despair that caused her to fail at all her endeavors.

Claire had other dreams that brought her even more in touch with her feelings. There was the dream, for example, of her mother giving her old clothes to Claire. In the dream, Claire doesn't want them, but accepts them because she is poor. Then she notices a beautiful tea set inside a cabinet. Claire tells her mother she wants it, but her mother refuses to give it to her. In this dream, being poor has nothing to do with Claire's financial status. It describes her inner impoverishment. The tea set represents the love that her mother withholds from her—the real reason why Claire feels poor.

Two months after her transformative dream, Claire had another dream, about a crippled man having to cross a stream in his wheelchair. His anger causes him to rise up onto his feet, and she falls in love with him. This dream was another version of her big dream, but there are two new and significant elements. She actually felt her anger in this dream. Her earlier dream feelings were fear and courage, not anger. Plus, she accepted and even admired this anger in her dream. Some people never approve of themselves expressing anger, and in fact feel guilty about it later. But Claire acknowledged, and, more importantly, loved the anger of her dream character, who was really herself. She realized that she deserved love and was furious that she didn't get it.

I want to share one final dream, which took place when Claire's husband left her for another woman. Her husband had married a dependent, timid, and subservient woman—as Claire was before she turned from mouse to tiger. But he did not want a tiger; he wanted a mouse. Did Claire take his leaving lying down? Not in the least. Although she grieved, she also realized that this was the best thing that could have happened to her. He was no longer the man she wanted, and he only held her back. In the dream, she was holding a fat, beautiful baby in her lap. When she first came to therapy her dreams of babies were sad—in one dream she found a dead baby in the glove compartment of her car. At that time, Claire's inner child was dying of neglect and lack of love. In her beautiful-baby dream, she was the mother to the baby within her, which in her dream was fat (well nurtured) and therefore beautiful. She had learned to love herself—in spite of parents who were not there for her and a husband who left her. She allowed the hidden self of her childhood to come out of the closet and into a room of her own. By opening up to herself, she was also opening up to the world. She began to get the recognition she deserved, because she valued herself.

Once Claire was on her own, she figured out a creative solution to supporting herself and her children, since her husband's alimony was meager. She did commercial paintings for money while painting for herself in a more meaningful way. Filled with energy and excitement, Claire recently commented: "I'm in demand, people seek me out, and I'm getting the recognition I never had before." Soon she will be having her first New York show.

Symbols for Your Dream Dictionary:

Tidal waves: Overwhelming feelings.

Black: Darkness, absence of light, depression.

Crippled: Impeded from fulfilling one's desires.

Wheelchair: Unnecessary support, compensation for and perpetuation of emotional handicaps.

Baby: The primal, unformed, innocent, helpless, dependent aspect of oneself.

Ocean: The unconscious. Our deepest instincts and passions. A symbol of rebirth.

Exercise: Write a Story from Your Dream

It's a shame we can't order a dream like Claire's, in which we are driven to take a dream action that changes our lives. But we can set the stage for these dreams by doing the dream exercises in this book. They will bring you closer to the actual feelings contained in your dream symbols and metaphors. As you get closer to your feelings and feel less afraid of them, you're more likely to let the true messages of your dreams come through. Plus, you won't need to defend against feelings in general. Here's an exercise you can do with your next dream, or an old dream that still haunts and perplexes you. Write a story that picks up where the dream left off and follow it to the conclusion. As you write, become aware of the feelings that arise. What interests and excites you about the story? Is there a conflict? The conflict is an indicator of your resistance and fears.

Margo, a participant in one of my dream workshops, wrote a story continuing this dream:

> DREAM: *I'm excited about a person whom I've recently met. I'm walking down Fifth Avenue thinking about him, and I see some yellow doves fly into a nearby tree. Then more yellow doves appear, hundreds of them, filling the sky and landing on all the trees in front of me. When I look up, all I can see are yellow birds. It is magical.*

Margo reported, "When I awakened from this dream I felt wonderful. The color yellow was so vivid in my mind. I knew these were birds that didn't actually exist, that I had invented them. I wanted to see where this dream led, so I continued it by writing this story."

> STORY: The birds seemed to light up my path. They told me that love was ahead of me, for they were yellow lovebirds. I wondered who sent them. Were they messengers from another realm? Were they sent by the person whom I was thinking about? I wondered what would happen if I asked one of them to fly down and land on my shoulder. So I went over to the nearest tree and asked the bird closest to me. He flew

gracefully toward me and gently perched on my head. Soon people appeared who looked at me in wonderment. I could see they thought I was enchanted.

I walked down the street, and whenever I saw something that disturbed me—like a beggar or people fighting, or someone who was upset—I would point to them and everything would suddenly right itself. The beggar was no longer poor, the fighting people embraced each other, and the upset person was filled with happiness.

I knew the bird had to return to its flock and was only mine for the moment. So I asked the bird if it could give me a gift in the form of wisdom. The bird told me to open my heart toward the new person I had met and to follow my dreams. So I did.

After I read Margo's story, I wondered about the significance of the color yellow. As I allowed the color yellow to surface within me, I experienced something pleasant, exciting and yet calming, too—unlike black. I experienced yellow as representing something mysterious, something that evoked pleasure and drew me to it. This made sense in the light of Margo's story. However, for Margo to decipher the exact message of her dream, she must explore what yellow means to her.

TWELVE

Murder on Stilts

The dreamer, whom I'll call Martin, was a highly successful creative director in a top advertising agency. He was well known in the business not only for his innovative ideas but also for his kindness, which was an anomaly in the dog-eat-dog world of Madison Avenue. He went out of his way to treat everyone with respect, and was unusually sensitive to the feelings of other people. The dream that follows, however, shows a completely different view of this man's psyche.

> DREAM: *I'm in a foreign country. I go to the post office and see a very tall man on stilts wearing a mask and cloak. He has a gun and he's killing everyone in sight. I run into a room for cover and hide under a table, hoping he will not see me.*

Despite his business success, Martin was not doing what he really wanted to do. His lifelong wish was to be a playwright, but he felt that would never happen. His parents had placed high expectations on him. They wanted him to stand out and be recognized as a leader in his field. Within the sphere of advertising he had certainly achieved success. But he'd have to be another August Strindberg or Eugene O'Neill in order to please them as a playwright. He felt he could never live up to those expectations.

Early on in his childhood, his parents noticed that he intellectually surpassed other children. They suspected they had a genius on their hands. They gave him an I.Q. test, and, sure enough, he scored well into the genius category. His parents doted on him. They thought his every comment and every action were remarkable and worthy of special respect. Martin was always the focus of attention whenever friends or other family members visited. His parents thought of him as "the little genius," someone who could achieve anything he wanted, able to devise solutions to problems that adults couldn't solve.

With those kinds of expectations it was no wonder that Martin thought he had to appear godlike to the world. In addition there were other reasons, of which he was not consciously aware, that made him feel he must not only be flawless, but also kind to everyone. His parents made it clear that appearance and performance were the top priority. Their unspoken message was that their happiness was inextricably tied to his success.

This was a tall order, especially since Martin's parents had seriously failed to meet his childhood needs. They were so focused on his performance that they failed to take care of, listen to, and nuture him. His mother was the worst offender. Martin had no idea when he entered therapy that he had been neglected as a child. He also had no inkling that he was enraged about this. His dream was his first clue that something was amiss. The dream also helped Martin see that his life was a masquerade. The dream's message startled him.

Martin wasn't happy when he first entered therapy. Initially, he came to me for couples counseling with his fiancée, Ruth. During our first session, Martin listened quietly while Ruth hesitantly brought up the issues that troubled her. Martin offered no answers or comments. He was tolerant but uninvolved. His attitude was unmistakably, *This is your problem, dear, but I'll indulge you.* However, midway through the session, Martin had a sudden childhood memory that brought tears to his eyes. The memory deeply moved him, but was so fleeting he could not remember what it was. In his previous experiences with therapy his feelings were never touched in this way. He realized something important had happened. It was because of that moment that he called me several months later to begin treatment.

His major concern at that time was that he had fallen out of love with Ruth. He did not know how to extricate himself from the relationship without hurting her. He was sure that the truth would damage her life irrevocably. He felt paralyzed—trapped by his guilt and yet tormented by his need to be free. He was convinced that he was living a lie because he couldn't tell Ruth that he no longer loved her.

In addition, he was not happy with his work, despite his apparent success. He wanted to write plays, but that was out of the question. It would mean giving up his high salary, prestige, and numerous perks for the likely possibility of falling flat on his face. His expectations were so high that he was defeated from the start. He couldn't even conceive of taking the steps required for this endeavor. If he were to write a play, it would have to be an immediate success. Since the chances of that happening were so remote, he refused to even try. He could not bear the thought of rejection and failure. His dream appeared unattainable. He was not willing to risk stepping down from his pedestal only to find that his perceived talent was just a fantasy. Above all, he could not risk betraying his parents' image of him.

Martin thought he gave everyone the impression that he was sailing smoothly through an enchanted life. He practiced Buddhist philosophy in an effort to be perfectly centered and calm. He avoided anger at all costs. One day as he was walking in the park with Ruth, some ruffians tried to grab her purse. Martin froze. Not only couldn't he protect Ruth and ward them off, he was unable to even speak. He did nothing while they manhandled her. When she picked herself up off the ground, more frightened than hurt, she angrily asked him, "Why didn't you help me?" Trembling as his heart pounded, Martin tried to hide his fear. He apologized but offered no explanation. When he related the incident to me, he admitted that he was ashamed of his cowardly behavior. He wondered why he felt such paralyzing fear. He hadn't been frightened like that since elementary school.

As a child, Martin had desperately wanted to make friends, but the other children ignored him. They sensed he could be easily hurt, so they taunted him. In turn, he learned to act tough to hide his shame over letting others see how easily he could be wounded. Martin also used his verbal skills to intimidate people and protect himself. His tongue could cut others like a sword. He kept his feelings buried and pretended nothing fazed him. But underneath his facade, he was quaking. No wonder he was terrified when threatened in the park; he had no real foundation of strength. The park incident was the first time he was consciously aware that he hid his fear behind a veneer of bravado. That event also illustrated how flimsy and superficial his successful image was. That was one of the messages of his turning-point dream.

Other childhood memories began to surface. He recalled the severe temper tantrums that started when he was two and continued far beyond the typical "No" phase of childhood. He and his mother vied for power by screaming at each other. These fights generally left him feeling frustrated and enraged and his mother feeling helpless and exhausted. Martin invariably insisted on getting his own way. Sometimes his mother gave in to him, and sometimes she held her ground. There was one battle he definitely won—the right to have ice cream at every meal. He simply refused to eat if it wasn't served. Martin may have won the ice-cream battle but he lost the war, because he still didn't get what he really wanted from his mother: the empathy and connection he needed. That unfulfilled need was the driving force behind the rage in his dream; i.e., the disguised man killing everyone in sight. Finally Martin resigned himself to the fact that he'd never get the love he needed. He stopped fighting, and by the time he was five he had turned into a docile, obedient little boy.

Even now, as an adult, Martin remained meek and mild, always charming to everyone. The notion of actually being angry at someone was way beyond his comprehension.

When Martin told me his dream, he couldn't make sense of the bizarre masked and cloaked man on stilts wielding a gun. His first association to "stilts" was his acknowledged desire to be high above everyone else. He also thought that being on stilts meant that he was off the ground, not grounded in reality. The stilts were a false elevation. Other than that, he couldn't identify with this dangerous figure at all.

The frightening character in Martin's dream could have stepped right out of a child's fantasy or nightmare, especially during that stage when children project evil characteristics onto monsters and other terrorizing figures. Dorothy Bloch beautifully illustrates this phase in her book, *So the Witch Won't Eat Me*. She explains, "Children's fantasies appear(ed) to concentrate on the fear of being killed, but the displacement of terror onto monsters and imaginary creatures was obviously designed to preserve an idealized image of their parents, from whom it was therefore possible to receive the love so essential for survival."

Was this what Martin was doing in his dream? Was he projecting his anger onto a monster figure in order to preserve parental love? Or was the monster a projection of Martin?

Before tackling that complex question, let's examine the subject of anger and why it is such a difficult emotion for so many people. Some people do not feel their anger, even when it's the most obvious and appropriate response to a situation. Others are afraid to express their anger, for a variety of reasons. Some common ones are: (1) the recipient of their anger would leave them; (2) the people who witnessed the anger would dislike them for their lack of control; (3) the anger would terrify others because it is as huge and powerful as God's wrath, capable of wiping out cities and destroying everything in sight. In fact, one patient told me that the reason why, in Greek mythology, Zeus is so often disguised (as a swan, for example) when he descends to earth is so that his mightiness and power will not frighten everyone away. The patient perceived his anger as so explosive that it could blow up several city blocks. Paradoxically, this patient often felt no conscious anger when people hurt or insulted him.

Back to the dream—what do the symbols mean? "Foreign country" implies an unfamiliar, perhaps dangerous place that only the unconscious mind has access to. What does "post office" suggest? A place where all kinds of communications are concealed (inside envelopes) and then dispatched from one person to another. The dreamer constructed a setting where the intention is to communicate something in a dangerous place, familiar only to the unconscious mind. Look at the dream character who shoots everyone in sight. Is he sending a message of rage? He is wearing a mask, a disguise meant to conceal his identity. The dream character is, in essence, faceless, which is another way the dream disguises the character's true identity.

As Martin and I discussed the dream, he saw himself as the perpetrator, the disguised cloak-and-dagger character on stilts. He talked about how he had to hide his vulnerability from others and elevate himself above it. He was forced to pretend he was above everyone else because, in reality, he felt threatened by them. He was sure his schoolmates would tear him apart if he did not demonstrate invincible strength. Eventually he learned to take this same stance with his mother. He acted superior and hid his own needs.

Martin assumed a benevolent disguise rather than an aggressive one in his waking life. The benevolence not only concealed his anger, but also expressed his awareness of other people's vulnerability and his dread of hurting their feelings, the way his could be hurt.

Where did this must-be-concealed ultrasensitivity come from? It was evident even before he entered school. A child who is loved needs little protection, for there is an inner strength that comes from that parental love and protection. Martin obviously didn't experience that kind of love, which led to the rage in his dream. That rage is expressed through the threatening figure of the masked gunman. This same rage caused Martin's childhood tantrums with his mother, which always ended in frustration. The gunman's mask is an interesting symbol. Since boyhood, Martin substituted a socially acceptable disguise—an air of benevolent superiority—for his true feelings of anger and hurt. In his dream, the mask conceals the dreamer, rather than his feelings.

The dream was Martin's only safe avenue of expression. A conscious feeling of anger was too threatening, for it challenged his self-image of an empathic person. Since his anger had to go somewhere, it came out in a dream, as repressed feelings often do. Martin now faced a choice: He could either dismiss the dream, which would be easy, or he could come to grips with its message. Martin chose the latter course.

Martin took us back to his first memory of anger toward his mother. In the present, Martin never criticized his mother. He felt it would destroy her. Suppressing his criticism served a dual function: (1) it protected his mother from his anger, and (2) it protected the feelings of all hurt beings, including himself. Remember how difficult it was for Martin to tell his fiancée that he no longer loved her? He was convinced that Ruth, like his mother, would be hurt beyond repair by the truth.

What kind of woman was his mother? She was, in fact, very much like Ruth—a shy, insecure person who depended upon Martin's admiration for her self-esteem. Our parents show up again and again in the people we select as our partners. That is often the reason why relationships fail, unless the participants become aware of what is truly going on.

Martin's mother was a beautiful woman. People sometimes stopped her on the street to ask her if she was an actress. Martin often spoke of her sensitivity, sweetness, and aesthetic sensibility that was never realized. He believed there was something quite special and unique about her. Although those are admirable qualities, Martin overlooked one crucial flaw. His mother's vulnerability was like that of a child. In many ways, she *was* a child. How does one cope with a mother who is a child?

Martin was particularly aware of his mother's fragility. She was shy and easily hurt. Martin's father often complained that their lives were too isolated. He enjoyed the company of others and felt it was good for his business to socialize with clients. His mother, on the other hand, was extremely uncomfortable in the presence of others. As a child, Martin remembered his parents fighting and his mother running into his room, as if to seek refuge in Martin's presence. Though only five or six at the time, he became his mother's protector. He always took her side during parental quarrels, thus alienating his father.

Martin was always conscious of his mother's state of mind. Was she comfortable or uncomfortable? Was she happy or sad? Was she pleased or disappointed? If she was unhappy, then what was he (Martin) doing wrong? What was bothering her? Martin was always prepared to defend her. But who was taking care of him? A child's focus shouldn't be on taking care of his mother. In fact, the situation was the mirror opposite of a healthy relationship. *He* should have been the focal point of her life, not the other way around. Martin's mother depended on him, and Martin consciously seemed to like this role.

What Martin failed to realize until it came out in his dream was that he was angry about not having his own needs met as a child. His mother was too fragile and incompetent, and she was not available to mirror his emerging self. In order to maintain his idealization of her, he had to brush away any awareness of her weaknesses. It would have been too frightening and dangerous for him to see her as the bumbling, disabled woman she actually was. His psychological safety depended upon his trusting this ill-equipped person. His denial took the form of overidealizing her beauty, her fragility, and her sensitivity.

Martin was delighted by his mother, and indeed she had some touching features. When he was fifteen, she sometimes helped him with his homework by reading to him at night. She loved to read—and escaped from her unhappiness through books. Whenever she read *Evangeline,* she cried. Martin never let on that he saw this, because he knew his mother would be embarrassed.

Martin's masquerade as a competent, godlike person was derived mostly from his assuming the role of the parent rather than the child. His mother lived through him, through his successes and failures. He almost felt as if he were living life for her, rather than for himself. He made sure he knew her wishes and fulfilled them. He felt her unhappiness deeply and longed to make it up to her by being her hero. What Martin did not see was that in certain ways he was just like his mother. She produced a son who, like her, felt unsure and unprotected in the world.

When we discussed the killer in his dream, it was initially difficult for Martin to identify with his anger. At first he felt compelled to furnish additional examples of his mother's endearing qualities. This unconsciously served the function of protecting her. He cried as he spoke of her unhappiness. Martin was genuinely sad about his mother's unhappiness, but he refused to look at the sorrow her unhappiness caused him. This repressed pain eventually caused Martin to acknowledge his anger, which is what he needed to feel to become authentic in his life.

Martin remembered another dream, one that he had when he began working at the advertising agency. He dreamed of a mother cat crossing a crowded street with a kitten in her mouth. The mother cat dropped the tiny kitten right in the middle of the street and left. Helpless and terrified, the kitten could have easily been run over. I asked Martin if he could identify with that kitten. He suddenly realized that his mother had indeed abandoned him. She had not given him the protection or inner strength he needed to survive in the world. Only his intricate, highly effective armor provided that, but there was a big chink in the armor.

As Martin began to feel his mother's neglect, he had more memories of his early tantrums. He also began to experience "irrational anger," as he called it, walking to and from work. He was irritated by the smallest things that people did. He wanted to kill a stranger who stepped in front of him on the street. I advised him not to stifle or run away from these feelings, even though they were uncomfortable. The anger was making its way into consciousness, a hoped-for result. On the other hand, I did not encourage him to act on these feelings.

One day Martin announced that he was enraged by the way he saw mothers treat their children. They wouldn't listen to what their children were crying about, they ignored them, or yelled at them, or stuffed something in their mouths—like the ice cream he had insisted on having at every meal, I thought. Martin was beside himself with anger as he reported this. This identification with those children was the first step toward feeling his own deep hurt. Once he could feel that, he could allow himself to be critical of his mother's incompetence. Martin was tired of being his mother's mother—or father. He made up his mind that his mission in life was to stop being her savior.

All of this took place over a period of months after the dream—and culminated in Martin's decision to take the risk of following his life's love: writing plays. He could support himself for a year or two on his savings and severance pay. To everyone's surprise and horror, Martin stepped down from his lofty position at the advertising agency and became a human being and a playwright. His fears about hurting both his mother and his fiancée lessened, and he finally broke off his engagement. This was his life, and he was determined to be the most important person in it.

Symbols for Your Dream Dictionary:

Foreign country: Unfamiliar territory, like the unconscious mind.

Post office: Place where messages are sent.

Mask: Hiding true identity and unacceptable feelings.

Cloak: Protective covering.

Stilts: Elevating, becoming bigger than real life, overcompensation, not being grounded.

Gun: Instrument of aggression.

Exercise: Find the Hidden Wish in Your Dream

Martin's dream was about disguises. Freud believed that all dreams were disguises of infantile wishes. The wish expressed in Martin's dream is a murderous one. It is quite the opposite of the way the dreamer envisioned his desires. Try to decipher the hidden wish in your dream. Be guided by all the feelings expressed in your dream. The other dream characters' feelings usually represent aspects of yourself.

Also ask yourself what this dream might be telling you, based on what you *don't have but want* in your life. Furthermore, is there a feeling expressed that is atypical of you (such as the mild-mannered Martin dreaming of a masked gunman)? Jung spoke of compensation dreams, which show a side of a person that isn't experienced in waking life. Jung believed the dream's function was to restore psychic balance. The dream provided what was missing in the person's life. So if you have a dream that shows you in a surprising light, one that is difficult for you to identify with, take a long look at it. Ask yourself if this could be a part of yourself that you are suppressing. No matter what messages your dream gives you, accept them as gifts. Your dream is like a loving guide who tries to help you see things about yourself that will enable you to lead a more fulfilling life.

THIRTEEN

Two Dreams of AIDS
Patients

(A) The Fisherman

Ken, a close friend who had AIDS, called me from the hospital and said, "Come over as soon as you can. I have a dream I want to tell you." I heard the urgency in his voice and hurried to his bedside. He told me this dream:

DREAM: *I'm in a wooded area by a lake. A friend I haven't seen in twenty years and who has since died breaks off a branch from a tree and uses his pen knife to scrape away the bark and create a smooth rod, which he hands me. I take it, attach a line, and sit on the dock waiting for a fish. Some men come along with fancy fishing gear and set themselves up to fish. They notice me and laugh. I feel a nibble on the line and see a small fish, which I catch. The men are still smirking. I put the line in the water again and this time a bigger fish takes my bait. I pull it in; it's quite a prize. The men, who haven't caught anything, watch me with interest. Then an enormous whale hurls itself up out of the water and winks at me.*

One of the most obvious features of this dream is its humor, but there are also other striking elements. The connection with nature, which implies immortality, is especially significant. Even though he was not a practicing Catholic, Ken probably recognized the Christian symbolism in the dream. For example, a fish is a symbol for Christ. In addition, a fisherman is one of Christ's disciples, who dedicates his life to working with others. Ken was in the last stages of AIDS at this time and was grateful for this healing dream.

Two days after he told me the dream, he was released from the hospital. He wanted to celebrate by taking his friends to dinner. He had been bedridden for weeks, and it took four blood transfusions that day to enable him to get up on his feet and walk again, albeit very shakily. He was looking forward to seeing all his friends together, perhaps for the last time.

That night there was a terrible downpour, accompanied by lightning and thunder. Because of the weather, his longtime friend Natalie asked him if he'd be willing to put off the meeting till the following evening. But Ken insisted it take place that night. No one pressed the issue, for they knew he was hanging on by a thread. They went to his favorite cafe and had a wonderful time, laughing and enjoying their strong, warm connection with one another. When it was time to leave, Natalie offered to walk Ken back to his apartment, which was a block from the restaurant. Ken stubbornly refused. It was important for him to feel he could make it on his own, even though he only had a meager umbrella to shield him. Unsteady on his feet, he slowly made his way home through the driving rain. On the way he met his hospice worker, who had been frantically looking for him. The hospice worker later told us that Ken walked toward him and announced that he did not feel well. Then Ken collapsed into the hospice worker's arms and died instantly.

Ken's dream was a declaration of triumph and hope. It expressed his belief in a universal order. The dream was transformational because it helped Ken come to terms with dying. It made him feel connected to something that was beyond, and bigger than, his individual life. Ken was at peace when he told me the dream, and I felt he was giving me two messages: one, not to worry about him, he was all right; and two, that the universe was with him on his transition to the next stage of his journey.

Central to Ken's dream was the water in the lake. Water is a symbol of life. On the night he died the heavens opened up and flooded the streets. It seemed like they were both saturating his world with life and weeping for him.

In his dream, Ken wore simple fishing attire and used a fishing rod that had been carved from a tree branch by a friend. This truly represented Ken, with his profound simplicity and connection to nature. By handing him the fishing rod, it seemed like this friend from the distant past was passing on a secret from a fraternal order. Why did this friend suddenly appear in Ken's dream? Was it to establish a linkage between life and death? Was he a messenger from beyond, since Ken knew his friend had died? The passing of the rod appears to be some kind of spiritual ceremony.

Ken cast the fishing rod into the water and effortlessly pulled up a fish, as if he was pulling some hidden knowledge out of the sea.

The men with the fancy gear scoffed at him. Their main concerns were appearance and performance. They laughed at something they didn't understand, and only stopped when they saw that Ken, without even trying, was much more successful than they. They could not do what Ken could do naturally. His success was not based on skill; it was based on a spiritual connection and understanding.

During his life, Ken was never successful in terms of wealth, acquisitions, or fame. He was a writer and artist who, in the view of some people, had difficulties keeping a job and supporting himself, although somehow he always managed. At times he felt like a failure. But his dream gave him another message—that he lived on a deeper plane, a spiritual one that was filled with joy and abundance. By not pursuing material wealth and success, he was open to this profound connection with spirit.

In his dream, Ken incrementally gained more and more knowledge, with the appearance of each larger fish. When the whale finally hurled itself up out of the water, Ken came face-to-face with the divine. The whale winked at him, as if to say they both shared a secret that no one else would ever know: death is not to be feared.

When I sat beside Ken at the hospital and listened to his dream, my only response was that it was a wonderful dream. Both he and I knew it needed no interpretation. Ken had been through a lot, and until now he had never discussed his religious beliefs. The dream not only expressed the depth of Ken's faith, it also reminded him of it. It prepared him for what lay ahead, and seemed to give him a great sense of peace.

Symbols for Your Dream Dictionary:
Lake: Place of reflection and insight; the unconscious undisturbed; a source of life.
Tree branch: Expression of creativity and growth.

Pen knife: Sharp, to the point, an instrument of skill and precision that reflects the user.

Fishing: Going into the unconscious to find its hidden treasures.

Fish: Symbol of Christ in Christianity, also the hidden treasures of the unconscious. Continual life.

Whale: The divine.

(B) Orgy Under the Table

John was a member of my dream workshop for people with AIDS. He was initially reluctant to tell this dream because of its sexual overtones, but finally put his fear aside and took the risk.

> DREAM: *There are three of us at a round table. I am underneath the table. The table is like a cocktail table in a bar or restaurant. It's away from the rest of the bar. Though I'm aware there are people at the bar, they are talking to each other and not paying any attention to us. The two other people at my table are a man and a woman, both of whom I know, but they have no identity in my dream. Everyone at the table is sexually excited, including me. Since I'm underneath the table, the people at the bar cannot see me. I'm very interested in the man. The woman is obviously masturbating, but it's unclear whether she's masturbating herself or the man. I feel sexually involved with the activity that's going on, but I don't think of myself as masturbating. I am very aroused by the situation. The woman climaxes at the end of the dream.*

The participants in the dream group helped John understand his dream by asking him what was on his mind the night he had the dream. They also inquired as to whether anything happened the previous days or week that could be related to the dream. This is what Freud called the "day's residues." John was very forthright about what had been going on in his life. Lately, he had been talking to his parents about his diagnosis and his recent symptoms. John had been terrified to tell his parents he had AIDS; he struggled for a long time before he got up the courage. In his case, as in others, his disclosure led to a closeness and love never before expressed between the members of his family. The one positive feature of AIDS, despite all its heartache, is that it has been a catalyst for love for many people.

Some of John's comments about his dream and his current waking life have sexual overtones. I have italicized them here because they were clues to the dream's meaning. He said, for example, that his conversations with his parents helped him *achieve satisfaction*. He told them much more than he ever had before about his life as a gay man. "My parents represent love to me," he reported, "and it's relieving to talk to them." He had been afraid they would be critical or reject him. He described his parents as people who were "not physical, *kind of sterile*, in fact. No one ever talked about personal things in my family," he said, "and I feel more comfortable now."

The dream revealed to John that he was getting the physical contact, pleasure, and emotional support he had never received before from his parents. He agreed that although the dream was shrouded in sexual imagery, it was really about achieving a loving connection with his parents—the two people in the dream whom he knows but who have no identity. (Dreaming of people without identity is a common dream disguise.)

After this dream interpretation, John wondered who the people at the bar were. During the week, he figured it out, and was eager to tell us at our next meeting. They were the members of his music group who did not know he had AIDS. He hid from them in the dream because he feared their rejection and disapproval. Becoming conscious of his love for his parents through the dreamwork gave him the confidence and courage to tell his music group his condition. He reported that instead of receiving the expected rejection and disapproval, he got just the opposite—love and acceptance. He was thrilled. Understanding his dream, therefore, helped him to take an action that markedly changed his life. He was able to make the transition from self-loathing and hiding to understanding and connection.

Having AIDS is such a life-changing event that many people reevaluate what is truly important to them. Because their time is limited, some people recognize that the immediate present offers their only chance of doing what they've always wanted to do. Many people come to realize that love is the most important thing there is. These people take risks they would never have taken before, for now they have less to lose. The fate they face gives them enormous courage and spirituality. Witnessing the love and understanding among people with AIDS can't help but transform all those fortunate enough to be involved with them.

Symbols for Your Dream Dictionary:
Three: Basic family.
Round table: Where those who share interests gather.
Bar: Place of self-gratification and escape.
Masturbation: Self-love.

Exercise: Act on a Message in Your Dream

When your dream gives you a message to do something, and it's something you want to do, then take the risk of doing it. Once John understood the positive message from his dream—the existence of parental acceptance and love—it encouraged him to go even further and do something he desired but feared: telling his music group, people with whom he already felt somewhat safe, that he had AIDS. He knew what he wanted—acceptance and love—and pursued it despite the risk of criticism and rejection. By listening to his dream and taking that risk, he got the love he wanted. This made an enormous difference in his life. His example is one we can all benefit from.

FOURTEEN

Dreams That Came True

I have saved a special kind of transformational dream for last—the prophetic dream. Not every prophetic dream is transformational; for example, dreams that foresee disasters or portray the sudden death of a loved one are not necessarily transformative. A dream is deemed prophetic if it predicts something that comes true. It is considered transformative if the dreamer undergoes a major change as a result of the dream. Sometimes the dream comes true without any effort on the part of the dreamer. In other cases, the dreamer follows the dream's message in his waking life, not knowing whether the dream will come true. Most dreamers are astonished when their dreams do come true.

Unlike most of the dreams in this book, the prophetic dream does not involve an obvious conscious struggle or decision on the part of the dreamer. For example, Patrick in "An Art Museum for the Blind" had to use his every last bit of energy to make his dream come true. Claire in "Crashing Through the Waves" had to make herself take the courageous step in her dream itself, and John in "Two Dreams of AIDS Patients" decided to fight his demons in his waking life. All of them achieved glorious victories from their heroic efforts. Now I am going to present seven examples of prophetic dreams that significantly changed the dreamers' lives.

In some cases, the dream's message was only a breath away from consciousness. In others, the messages appeared to be precognitive, previews of the future. In my opinion, these dreams are based on what Jung calls the "inner blueprint," the inner path that gradually unfolds in each of us on our journey through life. The dreamers followed their intuition, their feelings and hunches, rather than logic or reason. Since one of the primary messages in this book is to pay attention to your feelings and intuition, it is only fitting that we end the book with prophetic dreams. They are a reminder to carefully listen and seriously pay attention to your dreams.

1. The Beginning of a Fabulous Career

An actress, whom I shall call Louise, contributed this prophetic dream:

> DREAM: *I am with other actors, performing a play. Suddenly, a standing microphone, like the kind used in recording studios, appears before me. The next thing I know, I'm on the set of a live TV show, acting in a dramatic scene. Once again, a standing microphone appears in front of me.*
>
> *Both times the microphone is right in front of my mouth, as if I'm supposed to talk into it. The microphone has nothing to do with the story or production of either the stage play or the TV show. I keep dreaming this over and over. The last time I dream it, little cookies, Coca-Cola bottles, salt and pepper shakers, and elves dance around the microphone.*

In waking life, Louise was a theater and TV actress. The day after the dream, she got a call to do voice-overs for singing raisins, a loaf of bread, and several children. She had never done voice-overs for commercials before and actually knew very little about that side of the business. One of the commercials she did ran forty times a day on TV and the radio, and turned her, overnight, into a big voice-over star. Louise eventually did the voices for every one of the objects and elves who danced around the microphone in her dream. Her commercial revolutionized the field of advertising because it didn't specifically tell the viewer to go out and buy something. Instead it worked subliminally, showing a catchy, funny scene that consumers would recall when they went to the store and saw the product.

Writers from magazines and newspapers flocked to Louise for interviews. Her dream not only predicted that she'd become famous by doing voice-overs, something she had never even thought of doing before, but also specified some of the characters that she would ultimately portray. Needless to say, this newfound career completely transformed her life.

The dream was quite literal, for the dancing objects and elves were actual roles that she would play. Therefore, there are no dream symbols to explain or define.

2. The Secret of Life

A colleague of mine, whom I shall refer to as Lisa, contributed this dream. It occurred forty years ago, while she was under anesthesia for oral surgery. She claimed it was the most profound dream of her life.

DREAM: *I'm standing on a promontory, overlooking a huge valley. The view becomes unusually clear and everything appears sharper than normal—the air is cleaner, the vistas more distinct. I feel that I have somehow latched on to the secret of life, which is that life is beautiful.*

Then I find myself being torn away from this and pulled down beneath the earth. I'm lying on the bottom of a boat that's like a shallow hull. Two men in white coats whisper, "Don't let her look back and tell the others." I struggle to get free, so I can go back and tell everyone about my beautiful vision of life.

"The feeling in my dream was of deep regret that I wasn't able to savor the moment longer and share it with others," Lisa reported. "When the men in white appeared, I thought they were taking me on a journey to the netherworld. When I awakened I was absolutely elated that it wasn't too late to spread the news, for I was still alive. That state of heightened awareness of my surroundings lasted for several days. My vision seemed much sharper, the air seemed clearer, everything seemed more distinct and defined.

"The dream instantly made me more self-confident; it affirmed that life was good and offered a lot more than my habitual brooding indicated. Five years later, walking on the beach, I got the same feeling again. I was very aware of my strengths. I realized that the dream was the catalyst for a more positive way of perceiving myself.

"I've never forgotten that dream. I still experience that sense of clarity and beauty from time to time, usually when I'm looking at some vast beautiful landscape, such as the view from the Fifty-ninth Street Bridge, where you can see all the buildings in upper and lower Manhattan lit up. I get the feeling that I'm part of something immense and lasting."

The dream's prophetic message gave Lisa a glimpse of a deeper reality, one that she had never before experienced. This new vision was so profound that she now perceived life in an entirely different way. It caused her to struggle against death in her dream. It was not the demise of the body she fought against, but rather that of the spirit. The dream transformed Lisa's view of life—and made her want to share it so that others could benefit from her powerful vision.

At the time of the dream, Lisa had not yet chosen her life's work. I believe this dream unconsciously affected her choice, for she became a psychotherapist so that she could help others overcome the obstacles that prevented them from realizing life's richness and value. The dream was prophetic because it made her consciously aware of her wish to show other people that life is good. She fulfills her dream wish every day by helping her patients restore their faith in themselves—and in life.

Symbols for Your Dream Dictionary:
Promontory: Spot from which one can glimpse the world.
Valley: Enclosure, entrapment.
Vista: View into infinity.
Earth: Security, seeds of life. Also burial place.
Boat: Method of passage through the waters of life.
Men in white coats: Guardians of the ill and dying.

3. A Killing Before the Stock Market Crash

The dreamer, whom I'll name Justin, reported that this recurring dream made a huge difference in his life.

DREAM: *The recurring dreams consistently begin with me standing in a house or apartment that seems to have hundreds of rooms. I never recognize any of them. I am uncomfortable, because I don't know where I am and I always have a problem getting out of there. The last time I have this dream, something different occurs. Someone comes along and says, "You have to leave immediately or you'll be trapped here forever. There's only one way out." I say, "Show me that way," and the person responds, "It's over there, through the small hole that the rats use." I crawl out through the hole. Just as I get out, the building crashes down behind me.*

The next day Justin put his house up for sale. "That dream made me do it," he said. "The house was sold right away. What was so amazing was that someone bought it literally the day before the big stock market crash on October 19, 1987. If I had not put the house up for sale that day, I would have ended up trapped inside, just like in my dream. The house was one hundred years old. It needed a lot of work because parts of it were crumbling. No one would have bought it if they thought the economy was shaky, because there was no way to know how much it would cost to fix it."

Justin followed the message of his dream, just as Joan Witkowski followed the message in hers. Joan's message was written on a blackboard, while Justin's came in a precise, emphatic statement: "You have to leave immediately or you'll be trapped here forever. There's only one way out." The destruction of the building just after he escaped from it in his dream easily correlates to his selling the house the day before the stock market crash. In both cases, he would have been destroyed if he hadn't acted quickly. When messages are that explicit and urgent, pay close attention to them and seriously consider implementing what they tell you to do. But do act with caution as well, weighing all sides.

On another level, the dream also contained the message of moving from a stultifying place into a freer, better one. The dream indicated that the only way out was escaping through a small hole, which symbolizes birth. By having rats use that hole, the dream pointed out that the path to freedom might be scary and would require great will. Justin listened to his dream and took the staggering step of putting his house on the market, and, as in his dream, escaped just in the nick of time. Like the dreams in "Crashing Through the Waves" and "The Screaming Baby," it is the appearance of a new element in a recurrent dream that clarifies the dream's meaning or directs the dreamer to take a specific action that later proves to be beneficial. That new element is a manifestation of some significant change that has occurred inside the dreamer. In this dream, the crucial, new element is the voice that says, "You have to leave immediately or you'll be trapped here forever. There's only one way out."

Symbols for Your Dream Dictionary:
House: Self.
Hole: The womb; birth is crawling out of the hole.
Rats: Frightening instincts.

4. The Wise Man's Predictions

This dream occurred twenty years ago, when the dreamer, whom I'll call Alice, was living in Paris with her husband and two small children. She had this dream at a critical point of her life, for she had just decided to leave her husband and return to New York to go to school. This was her dream:

DREAM: *There is a large tent in the midst of a desertlike, Mediterranean location. It is very hot. I go into the tent and see a very tall, slender old man with a beard. He wears a long, flowing, multicolored robe with big sleeves. When I walk up to him, he tells me that I have three tasks that I must accomplish. Then he says, "I have something for you to take with you." I cup my hands and hold them out, and he places this little animal into my hands. It's a dream animal, not a real one. Soft and sweet, it curls up in my hands. I instantly fall in love with it. He also gives me a ring, saying, "This will help you through your trip." I wear it on my wedding finger.*

My first task is to get through the desert. While in the desert I use the ring, because it makes me feel connected to the wise man. I see his face in the ring. I also see his face inside myself. This connection with the man soothes me, makes me feel safe and supported. It gives me the strength to accomplish my tasks. I am accompanied by a little girl and I carry a little boy on my hip. They are the same ages as my children. The desert is very dry, like the Southwest in the United States. The ground is composed of red clay, with little scrub brushes scattered about. In front of me are huge red boulders. I know there are bandits in the desert, and the children and I have to hide from them.

Several different things happen during my adventure in the desert. Sometimes I am with both children, sometimes just one accompanies me, and other times I am alone. There are instances when I have a gun and other occasions when I am weaponless. There are periods when I hide from the bandits behind rocks. The desert is dusty, hot, and dangerous. The sun relentlessly beats down, and there is no water. I can't quit because I have to get to what lies beyond.

When I get to the end of the desert, the children are no longer with me. I have to complete my second task on my own. A gigantic dragon blocks my way. It's about three stories high, has little arms, and exhales fire. I don't know how I do it, but I manage to run past him without getting killed.

My third, and final, task is to swim a river. The river is fifty feet wide and the water is clear and cool, swiftly flowing from right to left. I dive into the water—it's wonderfully refreshing. I easily swim to the other side. I climb up the embankment and notice how lush and green everything is—the grass, the trees, the bushes, everything. The sun is shining and I'm in a lovely place.

"I had this dream twenty years ago, and it keeps coming up in my life," Alice said. "I'll forget about it for a while, but then it reemerges into my conscious mind. From time to time I still identify with one of the tasks in the dream. I find myself thinking, Now I'm in the desert phase, or Now I'm in the dragon phase. I think the desert phase is my childhood and adolescence, because I had such a depriving mother. It seems like the dragon phase has to do with relationships not working out. When I'm in a really difficult or painful relationship, I think, I'm definitely in the dragon phase now.

"In the dream I never stopped to question whether or not I should enter the desert, or meet the dragon, or swim the river. I just did it. That's pretty much how I try to live my life. Recently I had an operation. I thought to myself, I *want* to do this, so I'm just going to go ahead and do it. If I think about it too long, I'll never do it.

"It never occurred to me to *not* go through the three

tasks of my dream; that wasn't an option. The only question was *when* I would do it. The man was very kind. He reminded me of my grandfather. He had the same weathered face, he was slender, and he was old. My grandfather was not alive when I had this dream, but he was a very important, positive figure in my childhood.

"Lately I've been thinking a lot about the river in the dream. About six or seven years ago, I started thinking about spirituality. When I was a girl I turned to religion for solace. I went to church and read the Bible, and prayed every night. I had a good father up in the sky who loved me. Then I went to college and did a complete one-hundred-and-eighty-degree turn on the subject. I became completely agnostic. I poked fun at religion and laughed at people who were religious. But in the past six or seven years I've become fascinated with spirituality. It's a totally different approach to religion. It's put me in touch with my sense of expansiveness. It makes me feel safe and connected to life."

This fablelike dream was prophetic because Alice swam across the river to get to the other side. That represented her moving toward her spirituality, which is now a "current" force in her life. The dream also described her journey to another continent—from Europe to America—and all the hardships she had to endure to get there. The dreamer traveled from the desert, which was barren, to the lush green shores of life. The dream predicted, and even directed her, to rescue her life by leaving her husband and going back to school in New York. That act eventually led to the spirituality she embraced.

The dream was not just prophetic, it was also transformative, for it presented Alice with the obstacles she would have to overcome in order to change her life in this positive, meaningful way. It brought her in touch with her inner strength and strong determination to face life's difficulties. It also proved to her if she aggressively confronted each of the obstacles on her journey, rather than run away from them, she would make it to the other side—meaning not just survive, but also achieve something wonderful in her life. The dream gave her the courage to take the necessary actions, for it assured her that her goals were not just imperative but also possible. Alice took her dream's advice and followed that path. Ultimately, she didn't just survive that tumultuous journey, she also achieved a life that was far better than she could ever have imagined.

The wise man's ring gave Alice the faith to proceed with this extremely difficult rite of passage. The wise man symbolized her grandfather, and all the love and wisdom he gave her during her childhood. In the dream, her wedding ring was already off her finger. She put on her grandfather's ring, symbolizing her union with the loving, wise, parental figure, who would help her get through this confusing and sometimes painful period in her life. In short, the dream transformed her by teaching her to have faith and courage and to plunge head-on into each new challenge without giving it a second thought.

Symbols for Your Dream Dictionary:
Tent: Temporary dwelling.
Long, flowing multicolored robe: The robe worn by the prophet Joseph in the Bible, who made predictions through dreams.
Three: A mystical number signifying a whole.
Little animal: The instinct of love.
Ring: Symbol of marriage or union.

Desert: Place of despair, isolation.
Boulders: Obstacles.
Bandits: Soul robbers.
Dragon: Guardian of the path to enlightenment.
Fire: Path to rebirth.
River: Destiny.
Green: Color of life and of spirit.

5. The Opening of the Chakras

A woman, whom I'll call Elizabeth, had two prophetic dreams. The first one envisioned the opening of her energy centers, and the second one predicted her meeting the teacher who would guide her on her spiritual journey. She had these dreams one year apart, and claimed that the feelings they evoked in her were still very much a part of her life. This is her first dream:

> DREAM: *I am standing before my full-length mirror looking at myself. Suddenly a snake wearing a golden headdress appears in the mirror. He comes toward me and I turn around to face him. He looks as though he wants to tell me something. His presence is so powerful that I awaken somewhat frightened.*

"I told this dream to a teacher who leads spiritual workshops. He said it was an excellent, and deeply significant, sign of what was to come. The serpent, he explained, represented growth and movement. The teacher speculated that my energy centers (chakras) were ready to open, and said the snake was wearing the golden headdress in honor of the upcoming ceremony that would launch the deepening of my spiritual awareness.

"Since that dream I have felt stronger and more grounded, better prepared to make a commitment to my spiritual path. It created inside me a yearning for spiritual guidance—a teacher who would speak to my heart. I realized that I needed someone to help guide me to the next stage in my work and life.

"Finally I heard of such a teacher and arranged to meet him. I meditated prior to going to sleep the night before our appointment. The transfer of energy was more powerful than I'd ever experienced before. I was excited and afraid at the same time. That night I dreamed that my teacher (whom I had not yet met) came to tell me there was nothing to fear. I trusted him totally in that dream. When I met my real teacher the next day, he looked exactly like the teacher in my dream. This was my confirmation."

The appearance of the teacher in Elizabeth's dream was a clear indication that she should ignore her fear (which only made her retreat) and proceed with her plan. The teacher in the dream gave her a definitive way to confirm that the teacher she was meeting was the one she had been searching for. There is no easy explanation for how she was able to predict what he would look like, but both dreams were undeniably prophetic ones. Elizabeth told me that her dreams gave her the impetus to move forward on her spiritual path and were the catalyst for her current spiritual transformation.

Symbols for Your Dream Dictionary:
Mirror: Reflection of the true person.
Snake: Wisdom, healing.
Headdress: Ceremonial attire.

6. Metamorphosis

This dream both affirmed and clarified the transformation that had just taken place in the dreamer, whom I shall call Eric. Eric was a painter who had just undergone an unusual medical procedure. He suffered from a rare illness that affected his thyroid. The cure entailed a procedure known as the Transfer Factor, in which the doctor injected Eric with an extract made from his father's blood cells. Not only did the procedure produce physical changes in Eric, it also transformed his personality. Eric went from being supersensitive and moody, like his mother, to being talkative, affable, and even-tempered, like his father. Things that used to hurt his feelings now rolled off his back and sometimes even made him laugh. Eric had this dream shortly after the procedure was done.

DREAM: *A cockroach, the size of a young boy, walks out of my painting in my studio. I turn away in horror and see a woman, who I think is my mother, standing in the doorway. My mother, incidentally, hates cockroaches. I look back at the cockroach, which has climbed on to the venetian blinds, and watch as it turns into a black Labrador retriever.*

Shortly after the dream, Eric went to a social club and met a woman. Initially she seemed friendly, but suddenly, without explanation or provocation, she rebuffed him. In the past, Eric would have blamed himself and obsessed about the incident for weeks. But this time he realized the woman was eccentric and let the incident go. Needless to say, he was astonished and delighted with the new, easygoing attitude he had somehow developed. The dream predicted that his customary problematic relationships with women would become successful, rewarding, and enjoyable.

Eric's dream dramatized his unconscious feelings about himself and gave him the psychological insights required for change, which in his case happened without effort. Eric describes his painting in the dream as black and the rest of the dream setting as white. Like Joan Witkowski's dream, it presented its message in no uncertain terms—black and white. Eric created the painting, just as he created the cockroach that crawled out of it and the transformation that subsequently took place. The cockroach represented his unconscious feeling that he was so loathsome that even his mother hated him. Without knowing the dreamer well, one can only speculate what this means. Sometimes a son feels this way about himself as a defense against his oedipal rivalry with his father. It was only when Eric became like his father that he felt lovable. Consciously, Eric regarded the cockroach as his illness, as something repulsive and dirty. Eric clearly disliked the supersensitive side of himself. The fact that the cockroach was as big as a young boy suggested a further identification with Eric.

In the dream, the cockroach climbed on to the venetian blinds. The blinds symbolize deception and the inability to see something, for in reality they block out the light. Light symbolizes happiness, as well as clarity and truth. The cockroach climbed out of Eric's painting, which he created. This suggests that Eric believed that he gave birth to this aspect of himself, and thus blamed himself for it.

The cockroach turned into a Labrador retriever, an obvious symbol for love and affection. Eric's family owned a Labrador at the time, so that image also represented his family's ideal pet—a family member whose sole purpose was to give and receive love. This illustrated that Eric's newly transformed personality made him feel more lovable to his family. There are many psychological implications here, based on family identifications and rivalries. The main message, however, is that a major transformation took place in Eric, portended by a dream.

Symbols for Your Dream Dictionary:

Cockroach: Repellent, frightening.

Labrador: Loyal, loving companion.

Painting: Creation, reflecting the unconscious of the creator.

Studio: Place of unrestricted self-expression.

Mother: Representation of all women.

Blinds: Obstructions to truth and clarity.

7. A Waking Life Experience That Precisely Duplicated a Dream

"I was going through a very chaotic period when I had this dream," artist Margaret Evangeline explained. "A year later this dream came true. At the time I was writing my dreams down in a composition book, in an attempt to feel more grounded and secure. I wrote this dream down and added notes that clarified how the dream was related to certain experiences I was currently having. I studied the way my dreams' symbols and messages described what I was going through. This is my dream."

DREAM: *I am in a restaurant that's located in Baton Rouge, the city where I was born. This restaurant is about a block away from the first house that I ever lived in. As I enter the restaurant a woman meets me at the door. She appears to be the maître d' and owner of the restaurant. She speaks in a foreign language and I do not recognize her. I walk to the back of the restaurant and see an art class in progress. There are many students in the class. The teacher is someone I know who actually taught at*

Louisiana State University in Baton Rouge. I walk around and look at his painting of a horse, which he used to demonstrate a technique. I am surprised in the dream because I thought the teacher only did abstract paintings. I ask myself, "Why did he paint this horse?"

"One year after I had that dream," Margaret said, "a woman in Baton Rouge who had seen a catalog of my recent painting exhibition invited me to meet with her. She owned an art gallery and said she was interested in showing my work. I went to Baton Rouge to see her. The next day, when I returned home, I accidentally came across the journal where I had written that dream. I was astonished to discover that the dream predicted everything that happened in Baton Rouge. For example, the gallery was in the exact spot where the restaurant in my dream had been. In the dream there was an art class in the restaurant, and in waking life the restaurant was now an art gallery. The owner of the art gallery was a woman I had never met before, and she greeted me at the door the way the restaurant owner/maître d' in my dream did. She showed me around the gallery, and sure enough there was a painting by the same artist/teacher who was in my dream. She turned the painting around to show it to me, the same way I walked around to look at it in my dream. The most incredible part was that the painting was of a horse. I didn't remember the dream while I was in the gallery, and yet, just like in the dream, I said 'I'm surprised. I thought he did abstract paintings.' The woman replied, 'Yes, this is a big change. He's never done a painting like this before.' We both agreed that his new style was quite beautiful. It's really amazing how accurate my dream was. There was no way I could have known all of this ahead of time."

Margaret explained her relationship with her dreams. "My dreams are more vivid when I pay attention to them and write them down. I have a hard time remembering dreams when my life is chaotic. But if I make a practice of consistently writing them down, I not only remember them better, but I also find that their messages are clearer and it's easier to figure out what they're telling me to do. The solutions to my problems seem to automatically appear."

When Margaret discovered that her dream had predicted all the details of her visit to Baton Rouge, she realized for the first time what a powerful source of information dreams could be in both her work and her life. It affirmed for her that she could rely on some kind of inner wisdom that doesn't have to do with logic. She has trusted this inner wisdom more since her dream and calls upon it when she is making decisions.

Margaret had a successful art show at the gallery. And she was able to derive the full benefit of her dream because she had saved it by writing it down. The physical act of recording the dream also imprinted it in her mind and enabled her to unconsciously follow the cues in her waking reality that were related to the dream. She permitted, and even encouraged, a connection to form between her dreaming and waking lives. The strength of that connection determines how deeply and powerfully our dreams can transform us.

When someone is as connected to her inner life as Margaret is, it is not really that astonishing that dreams intermingle with her waking reality. Precognition seems to appear more frequently in those who are intuitively connected to life. We all possess the potential for precognition, but it is more accessible and developed in certain people. We can enhance our clairvoyant talents by increasing our involvement with our dreams. And as Swami Sivananda Radha says, "The more we act on the message of the dream, the clearer we get."

FIFTEEN

Conclusion

Aristotle determined that problem solving was comprised of four separate stages. The first stage is *preparation,* where the person defines the problem to be solved, then researches, reflects upon, and discusses it. That leads to the *incubation* stage, where the person's unconscious mind steps in and reorganizes and elaborates upon the data accumulated in the first stage. The third stage is *illumination,* where the person "sees a solution," has an intuition, a hunch, or a flash of insight. The fourth and final stage of the process is *verification,* where the person tests that solution by using it in the material world.

At stage two, *incubation,* a dream is born. At stage three, *illumination,* that dream is understood. A dream is a production of the unconscious mind. It is a flash of insight, an epiphany. Understanding the dream delivers the dreamer to stage four, *verification,* wherein lie the solutions and actions that can transform his life.

Sometimes an action is not required to solve a problem. There are occasions when all that is required is the insight or inner knowledge that changes the way the person perceives the world. For example, Mark, in "The Token Dispenser," was transformed when he permitted himself to feel his longing for his father, which he had blocked out until then. By experiencing that yearning, and the anger at being denied the support and closeness that he deserved, Mark's panic attacks no longer served a purpose, and subsequently disappeared.

When Peggy, in "The Wailing Wall," met a special person in her dream, she was finally able to acknowledge and appreciate her own vulnerability and wisdom. The special dream person was, of course, Peggy herself. That one act of self-acceptance transformed her entire life.

Joan, in "The Message on the Blackboard," heeded the words written on the blackboard in her dream, and was steered toward the work she was born to do.

Patricia's dream, "The Rapist at the Top of the Steps," taught her that her sexual problems were rooted in the way she tried to ward off death as a child. By investigating and reliving certain traumatic events, she was able to break the pattern that had prevented her from having satisfying sexual relationships with men for most of her life.

Beth met a person in her dream, "The Attacker," who never accepted her from birth and was the unconscious reason for Beth's overwhelming self-hatred. By recognizing the origins of her self-hatred, she was able to let it go.

Alan, in "My Volvo Disappears," discovered in his dream the source of his fear that nobody cared about him. He freed himself from that self-destructive attitude by exploring the emotions that caused it.

Marcy, in "The Monster in the Closet," directly confronted the fears that prevented her from having a successful career as an architect. Her dream told her what and who stood in her way, but she had to let go of her defenses and completely surrender to her feelings in order to gain this critical insight.

Jan's dream, "Under the Boardwalk," informed her

that her father behaved in an inappropriately sexual manner with her when she was a child. That realization put her in touch with her whole range of feelings toward him, from her disgust at his actions to her desire for his love. She was finally able to stop hating herself.

Patrick's dream, "An Art Museum for the Blind," transformed his habitual apathy into determination and success. The dream helped him give birth to the notion of a museum for blind people. The numerous, and substantial, obstacles that stood in the way of success were no match for his effort and dedication. Blind himself, he has created a whole new way for the blind to appreciate art and has provided the sighted with several novel artistic concepts. He is convinced that his love for this invaluable project has prolonged his life.

Angela's dream, "The Screaming Baby," caused her to see herself as a lovable person for the very first time. That insight transformed her by breaking her pattern of doubting that the significant people in her life really loved her. By allowing herself to fully experience the feelings in her dream, she was able to finally release her rage toward the mother who abandoned her during her early childhood. By releasing those feelings, Angela could relinquish her obsession with the other suffering creatures in the world—the abandoned, mistreated animals she frequently spotted on the street. Once she "owned" her pain by acknowledging and accepting it, she no longer needed to project it on to others.

Claire, in "Crashing Through the Waves," disrupted her pattern of being washed over and crumpled by life right in the dream itself. She established a new way of behaving when she crashed through the tidal wave. From that point on she abandoned her waking-life passivity and was transformed into an assertive woman who confidently forged ahead instead of retreating when confronted by life's many obstacles. Her life has evolved from merely being a struggle to survive into a rewarding experience that offers a multitude of joys.

Through his dream "Murder on Stilts," Martin discovered the true self that resided beneath his veneer.

Ken, in "The Fisherman," was blessed with a transformative dream that explained the meaning of life and ameliorated the difficult transition from life to death.

And as a result of his dream "Orgy Under the Table," John risked humiliation and rejection in order to get closer to others. He was rewarded with love and acceptance.

There is no doubt that the people in "Dreams That Came True," who were blessed with the priceless gift of prophetic dreams, were profoundly affected by their experiences.

Who has these transformative dreams, and why? Why do some people have them and not others? Many of us have transformative dreams but ignore them, thus cutting ourselves off from one of the primary sources of wisdom. "But not every dream leads to a transformation," you might argue. This is true. Big dreams do not come out of the blue. They usually appear after a lot of inner work has already been done. We are not always aware that this work has been done, because it can occur on an unconscious level.

Transformative dreams generally come when we are ready to hear them. We must want these dreams and their wisdom. Sometimes they appear when our defenses are worn down from either physical or mental suffering. Or perhaps we are in the midst of a confusing or difficult transition, such as the process of moving from adolescence to adulthood, or from adulthood to old age. We can be more open to receiving the truth about ourselves and our situations when we are especially vulnerable.

Dreams that occur during those occasions can help us heal. William Styron, author of the bestseller *Sophie's Choice*, lost his ability to recall his dreams when he was deeply depressed. Once Styron regained his ability to dream extensively and deeply, he awakened in the morning feeling as if he had been healed.

Dreams derive their healing powers from revealing the truths that we bury in our waking lives. Our dreams are like warehouses, storing our entire collection of personal truths. Some truths are difficult to look at, and others dazzle us with their exciting insights. Dreams can lift us to the height of happiness, as well as drop us into the chasms of our deepest despair.

It's helpful to learn how to decipher our dream messages. They often appear to be written in a foreign language—the language of the unconscious. When Joan Witkowski saw her dream message written on a blackboard, she paid close attention to it, even though it seemed to have no bearing on her life at that moment.

The best way to respond to a dream is to permit ourselves to feel the emotions that the dream has uncovered. This is the key to understanding the dream's meaning. Insights can come through intellectually interpreting our dreams, but real change occurs only when we relive the experiences that our dreams symbolically express. Oddly enough, dreams often disguise their messages so that we do not feel the pain. Like a loving parent, they wrap their insights in pretty packages to cushion the blow. If we want to get the precious gift inside we must open up that package by courageously plunging into the ocean of our fears and passions. It's human nature to avoid pain as much as possible, and one way we do that is by distancing ourselves from those emotions that threaten to hurt us. But ironically, the only way to permanently free ourselves from those painful feelings is by letting down the barriers we've erected to protect us and then allowing ourselves to fully experience every nuance of those emotions. To let go of a feeling we must first feel it inside us. Thankfully our psyches have a built-in mechanism that prevents us from feeling more pain than we can bear. Many people find that their feelings are not as hurtful as they imagined. That's because a lot of these feelings originated in childhood, when we didn't have the resources to cope with them that we now have as adults. Because we buried those feelings as children, we still perceive them from a child's vulnerable perspective. When we release them we discover that often they're not so overwhelming as we thought.

Dreams can do so many things for us—they can bring balance into our lives, give us creative ideas that we can implement, and enable us to face the truths that stifle us because they're buried.

Even though I have written about many dreams that seem to have caused instant changes, remember that the insights and wisdom that can transform us will lie dormant in our unconscious until we are ready to accept them. It took months for some of the dreamers in this book to fully understand, and implement, their dreams' messages. Major changes generally occur incrementally.

I am convinced that there are dreams that come from a level of experience that is not necessarily available to us in our conscious lives. That might explain the dream that Ken named "The Fisherman," or the dream of the teenager whose father had just died. Dreams give us glimpses into the unknown.

You can cultivate your dreams by acknowledging their importance, writing them down, exploring them in your mind, and doing the exercises presented in this book. In my own experience, I've found that nothing has the power and ability to transform my life as much as my dreams.

Chapter Summary

EXERCISE ONE
Walk Yourself Through Your Dream, Scene by Scene, Symbol by Symbol

Explore each symbol and action in your dream in the order in which it occurs. Let yourself experience the feelings behind these symbols and actions.

EXERCISE TWO
Ask for What You Didn't Get in Your Dream: Love, Support, Recognition, Forgiveness, etc.

Feel your need as completely as you can. Then imagine what it would feel like to be loved by the withholding person in your dream, or to succeed in a particular situation. Give yourself whatever you failed to get in your dream. What feelings, memories, and associations come up when you do this? Go with the feelings all the way and see how you feel then.

EXERCISE THREE
Dream Incubation

Before going to sleep, place a book, a pen, and a glass of water next to your bed. Sit quietly and think about a situation that troubles you. Then lie down and compose a question that addresses the problem. Repeat this question over and over in your mind as you go to sleep. Tell yourself to take a sip of water as soon as you awaken. Then write down whatever details or impressions you remember about your dream.

EXERCISE FOUR
Tell the Dream From Another Character's Point of View

Every character in your dream is usually some representation of yourself. By experiencing your buried feelings through another dream character, you'll both understand your dream and aspects of yourself you may have denied.

EXERCISE FIVE
Have a Conversation with an Important Dream Character

Ask the dream character specific questions like "Why are you in my dream?" and "Why did you behave the way you did?" When answering those questions, step into that character's shoes, so to speak, and write whatever pops into your mind. Don't censor or judge yourself or try to construct "logical" answers. Your immediate response is the most accurate one.

EXERCISE SIX
Give In to the Feelings You Awaken With

When you wake up in the morning with strong feelings (anger, depression, pleasure, etc.) from your dreams, give in to them and follow them, whether or not you understand what they're about. One way to pursue them is by writing them down. Another approach is to tell these feelings to a trusted partner or friend, to whom you feel safe confiding anything. Ask the listener not to interrupt until you are finished.

EXERCISE SEVEN
Go Back into the Dream

Find a place where you can safely scream, cry, yell, etc. as much as you want. Lie down in a comfortable position, preferably on a mat. Allow the dream to reenter your mind. Allow the feelings to come back to you. If there are no particular feelings, relax and ask yourself: Am I experiencing any physical sensations? What are the associations or memories that come up? Was there an earlier time in my life when I felt this way? What would I say about my feelings to the person or persons who evoked them? Where are my feelings leading me? What happens if I surrender myself to them and permit myself to express them?

EXERCISE EIGHT
Continue Your Dream While Awake

Continue the story of your dream to its conclusion. Let your thoughts, memories, and fantasies guide you and don't censor or judge what comes up. You can let a dream partner direct you, but those directions must come from you. One way to accomplish this is by writing down the directions and giving them to your dream partner. Follow the guidelines at the end of the chapter.

EXERCISE NINE
Listen to Music to Mirror and Cultivate Your Feelings

Most of us are better at hiding from our feelings than experiencing them. If we want to access the messages in our dreams we need to practice going with our feelings. When you want to be more in touch with both the feelings in your life and in your dreams, practice by turning on your stereo, lying back, and letting yourself be completely carried away by the music. You can also sing or dance or do anything else that deepens your involvement with the music and enables your feelings to run free.

EXERCISE TEN
Draw While You Tell Your Dream

You can do this exercise alone by thinking about the dream while drawing. Or you can tell your dream to a trusted friend or therapist while spontaneously drawing the most intriguing symbol in your dream. Examine the drawing. What does it tell you? What feelings does it arouse?

EXERCISE ELEVEN
Write a Story from Your Dream

Write your dream as a story, make note of all the feelings that arise. What interests you and excites you about the story? Is there a conflict in it? The conflict is a sign of your resistance and fears. Try to resolve the conflict in your story.

EXERCISE TWELVE
Find the Hidden Wish in Your Dream

Let the feelings expressed in the dream point you to your hidden wish. Don't rely solely on your dream self's feelings. The other dream characters' feelings are also important because those characters represent different aspects of yourself. Using the feelings contained or implied in the dream, figure out what wish this dream might be expressing. Ask yourself, What could this dream be telling me about what *I don't have but want* in my life? Are there any unusual feelings in the dream that don't seem to belong to me? If so, they could indicate unacknowledged wishes.

EXERCISE THIRTEEN
Act on a Message in Your Dream

If your dream gives you a specific message or instruction, and it's something you want to do—providing it's not harmful to yourself or others—take the risk of doing it.

Symbol Index

209

About the Author

Jill Morris, Ph.D., is the author of *The Dream Workbook* and *Creative Breakthroughs*. She teaches courses in dreams and creativity both at New York University and Cooper Union. As a writer and painter, she approaches dreams from a creative perspective as well as a psychological one. She leads dream and creativity groups as well as maintaining a private practice in individual and group psychotherapy in Manhattan.

David Morrell, born in Kitchener, Ontario, Canada, holds a Ph.D. from Pennsylvania State University and is now professor of American literature at the University of Iowa. First Blood was his first novel. He has since written a number of screenplays as well as A Fraternity of Stone, The Brotherhood of the Rose, The League of Night and Fog, and Testament. David Morrell lives in Iowa City with his wife and two children, and spends his summers in the mountains.